SMART PRACTICE WORKBOOK

Second Grade

PHONICS · READING · WRITING · VOCABULARY · MATH

SCHOLASTIC

New York ○ Toronto ○ London ○ Auckland ○ Sydney
New Delhi ○ Mexico City ○ Hong Kong ○ Buenos Aires

Text Credits: pages 42, 126–130, 137, 139, 144–145, 148, 152, 154, 157–159, and 171–172 taken from *Quick Practice Writing Skills* (Grades 2–3) by Marcia Miller and Martin Lee © 2003 by Marcia Miller and Martin Lee; pages 92–113 taken from *Handwriting Practice: Jokes & Riddles* by Violet Findley © 2010 by Liza Charlesworth; pages 114–123 taken from *Cursive Writing Practice: Jokes & Riddles* by Violet Findley © 2010 by Liza Charlesworth; pages 131, 141, 153, 163, 166, and 170 taken from *40 Elaboration Activities That Take Writing From Bland to Brilliant!* (Grades 2–4) by Martin Lee and Marcia Miller © 2007 by Martin Lee and Marcia Miller; pages 132–136, 138, 140, 142, 146–147, 149–150, and 160–162 taken from *Instant Grammar Practice Kids Will Love* (Grades 2–3) by Linda Ward Beech © 2010 by Linda Ward Beech; pages 164–165 and 167–169 taken from *Writing Lessons to Meet the Common Core* (Grade 2) by Linda Ward Beech © 2013 by Linda Ward Beech; pages 230, 232, 285–286, 297, and 306–307 taken from *25 Common Core Math Lessons for the Interactive Whiteboard* (Grade 2) by Steve Wyborney © 2014 by Steve Wyborney.

Other pages from this workbook were previously published in: *Morning Jumpstarts: Reading* (Grade 2), *Quick Cloze Passages for Boosting Comprehension* (Grades 2–3), *Hi-Lo Nonfiction Passages for Struggling Readers*, *25 Complex Text Passages to Meet the Common Core: Literature and Informational Texts* (Grade 2), *240 Vocabulary Words Kids Need to Know* (Grade 2), *Morning Jumpstarts: Math* (Grade 2), and *50+ Super-Fun Math Activities* (Grade 2).

Editor: Maria L. Chang
Cover design by Michelle Kim
Cover art by Constanza Basaluzzo
Interior design by Adrienne Downey

Photos ©: 44: Onfokus/iStockphoto; 46 top: stevelenzphoto/iStockphoto; 46 bottom: paytai/iStockphoto; 48 top: Balashark/iStockphoto; 50 top: lzf/Shutterstock, Inc.; 50 bottom: rimglow/iStockphoto; 52: samvaltenbergs/iStockphoto; 54: sinopics/iStockphoto; 56: Alfred Russell/Corbis Images; 58: RUBE GOLDBERG ® is a registered trademark of Rube Goldberg Inc., All materials used with permission.; 62 top: ilbusca/iStockphoto; 62 bottom: MoreISO/iStockphoto; 66: Everett Historical/Shutterstock, Inc.; 76: Thomas Kristich, 2008.

Illustrations by Teresa Anderko, Delana Bettoli, Maxie Chambliss, Rusty Fletcher, Mike Gordon, James Graham Hale, Doug Jones, Anne Kennedy, Mike Moran, Maggie Smith, Bari Weissman, and Sydney Wright

ISBN: 978-0-545-86253-0

6 7 8 9 10   68   23 22 21

Dear Parent,

The fact that you're holding this book in your hands strongly indicates that you care very much about your child's learning and want him or her to succeed in school. Well, you've made the right choice in picking this workbook. The Scholastic brand is well known for high-quality educational materials for use in schools and at home. Inside you'll find hundreds of engaging practice pages designed to boost your child's skills in reading, writing, math, and more.

Smart Practice Workbook: Second Grade is divided into six sections: Phonics, Reading Comprehension, Handwriting, Grammar & Writing, Vocabulary, and Math. The table of contents lists the specific skills your child will be practicing on each page. Feel free to move through the pages in any order you wish. An answer key is provided in the back so you can check your child's progress.

To help your child get the most out of the learning experience offered in this book, try these quick tips:

- Provide a comfortable and quiet place for your child to work.

- Make sure your child has all the supplies he or she needs, such as pencils, crayons, or markers.

- Keep work sessions short, but frequent. For a child in second grade, 20 minutes each day is sufficient.

- Encourage your child's efforts, praising his or her successes and offering positive help when your child makes a mistake.

All set? Then let's get started on this journey to helping your child become a successful, lifelong learner.

-The Editors

Grade-Appropriate Skills Covered in
Smart Practice Workbook: Second Grade

LANGUAGE ARTS

- Know and apply grade-level phonics and word analysis skills in decoding words.

- Recognize and read grade-appropriate irregularly spelled words.

- Ask and answer such questions as *who, what, where, when, why*, and *how* to demonstrate understanding of key details in a text.

- Describe the overall structure of a story, including describing how the beginning introduces the story and the ending concludes the action.

- Identify the main topic of a multiparagraph text as well as the focus of specific paragraphs within the text.

- Identify the main purpose of a text, including what the author wants to answer, explain, or describe.

- Read with sufficient accuracy and fluency to support comprehension.

- Print all uppercase and lowercase letters in manuscript and cursive.

- Demonstrate command of the conventions of standard English grammar and usage when writing.

- Produce, expand, and rearrange complete simple and compound sentences.

- Demonstrate command of the conventions of standard English capitalization, punctuation, and spelling when writing.

- Use appropriate end punctuation for sentences.

- Write informative/explanatory texts in which the student introduces a topic, uses facts and definitions to develop points, and provides a concluding statement or section.

- Write narratives in which the student recounts a well-elaborated event or short sequence of events.

- Use sentence-level context as a clue to the meaning of a word or phrase.

- Determine the meaning of the new word formed when a known prefix is added to a known word (e.g., happy/unhappy, tell/retell).

MATH

- Represent and solve problems involving addition and subtraction.

- Work with addition and subtraction equations.

- Understand place value.

- Use place value understanding and properties of operations to add and subtract.

- Identify fractions.

- Work with equal groups of objects to gain foundations for multiplication.

- Measure and estimate lengths in standard units.

- Work with time and money.

- Represent and interpret data.

- Reason with shapes and their attributes.

Table of Contents

Phonics

Reading Comprehension

Handwriting

Grammar & Writing

Vocabulary

Math

Using the Flash Cards

At the back of this book are ready-to-use flash cards featuring selected words from the Vocabulary section of this workbook. Some of these are words that we use every day in conversation, while others are related to specific content areas, such as science, math, or social studies. Learning these words and their meanings will help increase your child's reading comprehension as well as his or her oral communication and writing skills. Here are a few tips to make the most of these vocabulary flash cards:

- Introduce up to ten new words at a time. Choose a word card and have your child read the word aloud. Alternatively, you could read the word then have your child repeat it after you. Next, ask your child if he or she knows the meaning of the word. Encourage your child to explain what he or she thinks the word means. Then turn the card over and read the definition together. Is the definition close to what your child thought the word means? Invite your child to use the word in a sentence. You might also ask your child to think of another word that reminds him or her of the vocabulary word, because it either means the same thing or the opposite, or because the words are related somehow. Repeat with the remaining word cards.

- Once you have reviewed all the word cards, test your child's knowledge by reading the definition side and saying "blank" in place of the boldfaced word. For example, "A *blank* is a very heavy snowstorm." Ask your child to name the missing word (*blizzard*). For an added challenge, you might ask your child to spell the missing word.

- Invite your child to sort the word cards into different categories; for example, weather words or character traits. Here are some other ways your child could sort the words:
  - alphabetical order
  - number of syllables
  - vowel sounds (words with long-*e* or short-*i* sounds)
  - parts of speech (noun, verb, or adjective)

  You could also invite your child to come up with his or her own categories for sorting the cards.

- Use the vocabulary cards to play charades or quick draw. Place the word cards in a paper bag. Take turns picking a word card and either draw it on a large sheet of paper or act it out for the other person to guess. Give a bonus point if the guesser can also spell the word correctly.

A **brave** person acts strong and without fear.

brave

Phonics

10

Name each picture.
Write the letter that stands for the **beginning** sound.

1. _____

4. _____

2. _____

5. _____

3. _____

6. _____

Name each picture.
Write the letter that stands for the **ending** sound.

1. _____

4. _____

2. _____

5. _____

3. _____

6. _____

Name each picture.
Write the letter that stands for the **middle** sound.

1. _____

2. _____

3. _____

4. _____

5. _____

6. _____

Where's the **T** in each word? Name each picture. Listen for its **T** sound. Write **B** for *beginning*, **M** for *middle*, or **E** for *end*.

1. _____

2. _____

3. _____

4. _____

5. _____

30

6. _____

Write **m**, **n**, or **r** to complete each word.

1. lu _____ p

5. _____ oise

2. sc _____ ap

6. _____ arble

3. fi _____ d

7. drai _____

4. fil _____

8. _____ attle

Fill in the missing vowels. Use the letter bank.
Read the words.

1. b _____ lt

4. b _____ ll

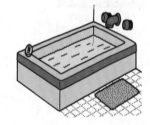

2. b _____ th

5. b _____ ll

3. b _____ ll

6. b _____ g

Write two different words for each short-*a* word family.
One is done for you.

-ack	-ap
black	
-ank	**-ash**
-at	**-an**

Write two different words for each short-*e* word family.
One is done for you.

-ell	-ent
well	

-est	-ess

-eck	-ed

Write two different words for each short-*i* word family.
One is done for you.

-ick	-ink
brick	well

-ill	-itch

-ing	-ig

Write two different words for each short-*o* word family.
One is done for you.

-ock	-og
block	duck

-op	-ox

-ob	-ot

Write two different words for each short-*u* word family.
One is done for you.

-uck	-unk
duck	

-ug	-ush

-ump	-ub

Read each word pair. Circle pairs that rhyme.

1. fix   box

5. pink   prince

2. weep   deep

6. arch   birch

3. Fred   bread

7. bench   French

4. grab   glad

8. swift   lift

Cross out the word that does *not* have a long-*a* sound.
Then write a new word that uses the same sound.

1. bake   lake   can   _____

2. pan   mail   nail   _____

3. clay   tray   had   _____

4. gal   grate   date   _____

Cross out the word that does *not* have a long-e sound.
Then write a new word that uses the same sound.

1. sell   deal   steal _____

2. bend   free   three _____

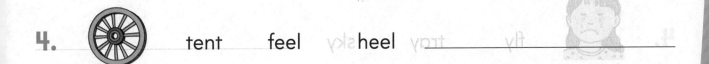
3. bleed   feed   set _____

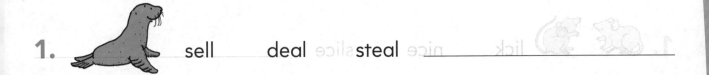
4. tent   feel   heel _____

Cross out the word that does *not* have a long-*i* sound.
Then write a new word that uses the same sound.

1. 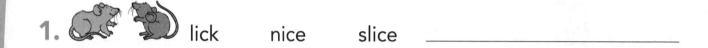 lick   nice   slice   _____

2.  hide   bread   wide   _____

3.  light   fright   kit   _____

4.  fly   tray   sky   _____

Cross out the word that does *not* have a long-o sound.
Then write a new word that uses the same sound.

1.  coat   float   box   _____

2. 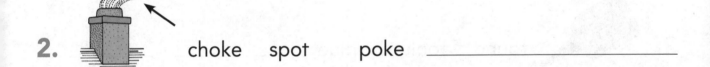 choke   spot   poke   _____

3. 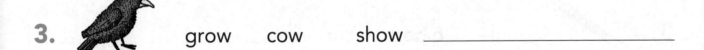 grow   cow   show   _____

4. phone   stone   bun   _____

Circle the word that *has* a long-*u* sound.
Then write a new word that uses the same sound.

1.  hub   tube   cub   _____

2.  round   took   blue   _____

3.  mute   blood   cut   _____

4. 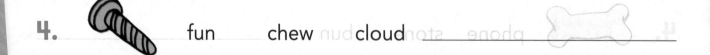 fun   chew   cloud   _____

Circle the correct spelling of the word for each picture.
Then copy it.

1.  soot   sut   suit   _____

2.   to   two   too   _____

3.  roof   rough   rewf   _____

4.  sup   soup   soop   _____

Read each word in the word bank.
Write it where it goes in the vowel chart.

Long *a*

Long *e*	Long *i*

Long *o*	Long *u*

The letters **oo** can have two different sounds.
o͞o stands for long *oo*, as in **m<u>oo</u>n**.
o͝o stands for short *oo*, as in **b<u>oo</u>k**.
Say each word in the word bank.
Write it in the chart where it belongs.

Word Bank

cook	spoon
fool	foot
hood	room
school	good
tooth	look

o͞o as in *moon*	o͝o as in *book*

Each sentence below needs an *-ar* word and an *-or* word.
Read the words in boldface. Write them in the blanks
so each sentence makes sense.

1. car   shore

Al drove the _____ to the sea _____.

2. sharp   thorns

The _____ on a rose are very _____.

3. farm   corn

We pick _____ at a local _____.

4. hard   sport

Is the _____ of golf _____ for kids?

5. smart   horse

How do I know if a _____ is _____?

Each word in the word bank has an **/ur/** sound spelled with ***-er***, ***-ir***, or ***-ur***.
Write each word in the chart where it belongs.

Word Bank

girl	fern
germ	fur
stir	hurt
curl	shirt
burn	verb
first	serve

h<u>er</u>d

b<u>ir</u>d

n<u>ur</u>se

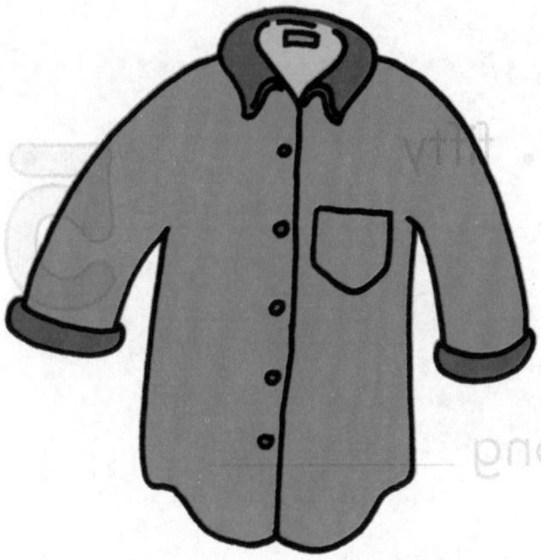

When **y** is a vowel, it can sound like **long e** or **long i**.
Read each word. Write **e** or **i** to tell which sound of **y** you hear.

1. fly

long _____

5. cry

long _____

2. fifty

long _____

6. dry

long _____

3. jelly

long _____

7. strawberry

long _____

4. sky

long _____

8. baby

long _____

The *schwa* /ə/ is a quick sound with no accent.
Schwa has the **/uh/** sound, as in **alone**.
Circle the word in each pair that begins with the schwa sound.

1. alarm   acted

2. anger   again

3. adding   adult

4. agree   ashes

5. asking   awake

6. asleep   army

7. aim   ago

8. able   about

C can have two different sounds. Soft *c* sounds like /s/, as in <u>c</u>ity. Hard c sounds like /k/, as in <u>c</u>amp. Read each word. Write **S** or **H** to show whether you hear a **S**oft *c* or **H**ard *c*.

1. cup _____

5. camel _____

2. celery _____

6. fence _____

3. cow _____

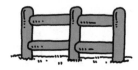

7. claw _____

4. ice _____

8. candle _____

G can have two different sounds. Soft *g* sounds like /j/, as in **gentle**. Hard *g* sounds like /g/, as in **game**. Read each word. Write **S** or **H** to show whether you hear a **S**oft *g* or **H**ard *g*.

1. guitar _____

5. cage _____

2. giraffe _____

6. bridge _____

3. giant _____

7. gem _____

4. goose _____

8. glass _____

Write an exact rhyme for each word below.
Start with an **r blend** from the box.
Use each blend at least once.

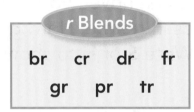

r Blends

br	cr	dr	fr
	gr	pr	tr

1. doom _____

2. mesh _____

3. wisp _____

4. book _____

5. lift _____

6. tapes _____

7. must _____

8. thank _____

On each blank, write an ***l* blend** from the box
to make a word. Use each blend at least once.

l Blends		
bl	cl	fl
gl	pl	sl

1. _____ ace   5. _____ eep

2. _____ ea   6. _____ ick

3. _____ ove   7. _____ oom

4. _____ ade   8. _____ ue

Solve each riddle by writing
a word that starts with an
s blend from the box.

s-blend words			
scare	slow	smart	small
spoil	star	swim	sleeve

1. Not large?

_____

2. Move in water?

_____

3. Part of a shirt?

_____

4. Sky twinkler?

_____

5. Say boo!

_____

6. Go bad?

_____

7. Knows a lot?

_____

8. Not fast?

_____

Copy the word for each picture. Underline its **final blend**.

1. dusk
desk
disk

_____

2. gust
grant
gift

_____

3. stamp
stump
scalp

_____

4. cold
cord
colt

_____

5. quiet
quart
quilt

_____

6. held
hump
hand

_____

7. drink
drift
dump

_____

8. test
tent
tend

_____

9. bird
boast
board

_____

10. stark
short
shark

_____

11. chunk
chest
champ

_____

12. wart
wasp
wind

_____

Write the **beginning** consonant digraph so that each phrase makes sense.

1. fried _____ icken

2. window _____ ade

3. dad's cell _____ one

4. ten, twenty, _____ irty

5. when and _____ ere

6. _____ ow and tell

Write the **ending** consonant digraph so that each sentence makes sense.

Consonant Digraphs

ch   gh   ng   ph   sh   th

7. My cold makes me cou _____.

8. A bar gra _____ shows data.

9. What a juicy pea _____!

10. Let's si _____ a lively tune.

11. Mario lost another too _____.

12. Please feed the goldfi _____.

Circle all the words that have the **/oy/** sound.

1. boil   olive   enjoy   port   point

....

2. royal   coin   body   voice   small

....

3. Joyce   Troy   Leon   Leroy   Cody

....

Circle all the words that have the **/ow/** sound.

4. shout   coach   howl   cloud   grown

....

5. meow   crown   flute   pout   flower

....

6. allow   ouch   pillow   show   loud

....

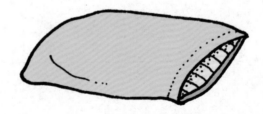

Write a word that begins with the same sound as each picture does.

1. _____

2. _____

3. _____

4. _____

5. _____

6. _____

7. _____

8. _____

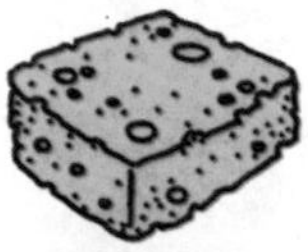

9. _____

10. _____

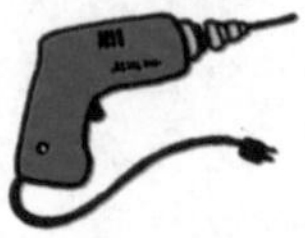

Reading Comprehension

The Mystery of the Great Stones

In many places around the world, there are large blocks of stone. Some of these stand alone. Others form rings or lines. Still others look like huge tables. They are some of the earliest buildings.

Most of these stones are on flat land. No other stones are around them. We think people from long ago used ropes and logs to move the stones. This took many years.

What did the stones mean? It's still a mystery. Some rings may have been calendars. Maybe they were meeting places. What do you think?

Stonehenge, England

Fill in the letter with the best answer for each question.

1. What might a ring of stones have looked like to the builders?

   Ⓐ the sun

   Ⓑ a tree

   Ⓒ a person

2. Which word best tells about the builders of the stone groups?

   Ⓐ small

   Ⓑ clever

   Ⓒ hungry

3. These groups of stones are some of the first

   Ⓐ tables.

   Ⓑ mountains.

   Ⓒ buildings.

4. What is the mystery of the great stones?

   Ⓐ why people made the stone buildings

   Ⓑ how many stone buildings were made

   Ⓒ what a ring of stones looks like

S-S-S-Snakes!

Some snakes live in forests. Some live in hot, dry deserts. Others live in lakes or streams. Some snakes even live in the sea! Some snakes live almost everywhere. But they never live where it is always freezing cold.

Most snakes are harmless to people. However, they will attack animals that threaten them. Some snakes have skin patterns that make them hard to see. Others make noises to scare off enemies. Certain snakes "play dead" to stop an attack.

Snakes use their long tongues to smell things. They shed their skin as they grow. And they never close their eyes to sleep!

Fill in the letter with the best answer for each question.

1. What is the main idea of the article?

Ⓐ Snakes can live in trees.

Ⓑ Snakes live almost everywhere.

Ⓒ Snakes do not like freezing cold weather.

2. Which is a detail from the article?

Ⓐ The author does not like snakes.

Ⓑ Some snakes live in the sea.

Ⓒ Snakes never go underground.

3. Snakes cannot live

Ⓐ where it is always very cold.

Ⓑ in forests.

Ⓒ in lakes or streams.

4. If an attacker saw a snake that was not moving, it would probably

Ⓐ bury it in the ground.

Ⓑ eat it quickly.

Ⓒ leave it alone.

An 8,000-Mile Shortcut!

Suppose a ship wants to sail from New York to California. One route takes many weeks. Another sails through the Panama Canal. It is an 8,000-mile shortcut for ships!

The Panama Canal is only about 50 miles long. But it took ten years to build! Workers had to dig all across Panama. They hauled away tons of dirt. It was not easy to dig through jungles, hills, and swamps.

Insects were a big problem. Some spread yellow fever and other diseases. To kill the insects, workers drained swamps and cleared brush. It was a hard job, but it worked! In 1914, workers finished the canal.

Fill in the letter with the best answer for each question.

1. Why was the Panama Canal built?

   Ⓐ to give workers something to do

   Ⓑ to have tons of dirt to haul away

   Ⓒ to make a shorter way for ships to travel

2. Insects were a problem because they

   Ⓐ spread disease to workers.

   Ⓑ drank water.

   Ⓒ didn't want the canal finished.

3. How did workers get rid of harmful insects?

   Ⓐ They drowned them.

   Ⓑ They drained swamps and cleared brush.

   Ⓒ They dug them up.

4. Which statement is true?

   Ⓐ The Panama Canal is a shorter route.

   Ⓑ The Panama Canal is a longer route.

   Ⓒ The Panama Canal is a more dangerous route.

Planting a Vegetable Garden

Summer is the time to plant vegetables like peas, corn, and peppers. Planting a vegetable garden is easy. Here's how:

1. Turn the soil.
Turn the earth over with a rake. Roots grow better in loose soil. They can grow down into the ground.

2. Plant the seeds.
Plant the seeds in rows. Cover the seeds with soil.

3. Water the plants.
Plants need water and sunlight to grow. Water your plants when the soil is dry.

4. Pull the weeds.
Pull out any wild, unwanted plants. They use soil and water that your other plants need to grow.

5. Pick and eat your vegetables!

Fill in the letter with the best answer for each question.

1. What is the first thing you need to do to plant a vegetable garden?

   Ⓐ pick the vegetables

   Ⓑ turn over the soil

   Ⓒ plant the seeds

2. After putting the seeds in rows, what is the next step?

   Ⓐ watering the plants

   Ⓑ covering the seeds with soil

   Ⓒ picking and eating the vegetables

3. What helps the vegetable plants grow?

   Ⓐ water and sunlight

   Ⓑ weeds and bugs

   Ⓒ milk and eggs

4. The main thing this story tells about is

   Ⓐ life on a farm.

   Ⓑ big, funny vegetables.

   Ⓒ how to grow vegetables.

Waves for You

Here's the problem: You love to play in the waves, but you don't live near the sea. You also don't like jellyfish or seaweed! Maybe you hate getting knocked over when the ocean is rough.

What can you do? You can go to a wave pool! Wave pools look like normal swimming pools, but they're not.

Special machines make waves that can be turned on and off. Sometimes the waves are gentle. Then you can swim or float. At other times, the waves are big and wild!

Some wave pools even have beaches or slides. Find one near you—and have fun!

Fill in the letter with the best answer for each question.

1. Wave pools look like other swimming pools but they

    Ⓐ are far away.

    Ⓑ have beaches.

    Ⓒ have waves that can be turned on and off.

2. How are wave pools different from the ocean?

    Ⓐ They do not have jellyfish.

    Ⓑ They can have big waves.

    Ⓒ They have seaweed.

3. The waves in a wave pool are made by

    Ⓐ the sea.

    Ⓑ machines.

    Ⓒ swimmers.

4. The author thinks that wave pools are

    Ⓐ a fun place to go.

    Ⓑ not safe.

    Ⓒ full of sharks.

The Great Wall of China

What's the biggest wall you've ever seen? Is it about 30 feet tall? Is it thousands of miles long? Probably not. There's only one wall that big. It's the Great Wall of China.

Two thousand years ago, China had many enemies. The emperor thought a strong wall would keep China safe. He had people mend old walls. He had them build new ones out of stone and mud. Then they connected all the walls into one great wall. It was 3,000 miles long!

For the next 1,000 years, other emperors extended the wall. Finally, it stretched for more than 13,000 miles. Much of it still stands today.

Fill in the letter with the best answer for each question.

1. Which event happened first?

Ⓐ New walls were connected to old walls.

Ⓑ People mended old walls.

Ⓒ The emperor decided to build the wall.

2. Which event happened last?

Ⓐ Old walls and new walls were connected.

Ⓑ Other emperors extended the wall.

Ⓒ China had many enemies.

3. The building of the Great Wall began

Ⓐ about 2,000 years ago.

Ⓑ two years ago.

Ⓒ about 20 years ago.

4. Which statement is a fact?

Ⓐ The Great Wall was more than 13,000 miles long.

Ⓑ Building the Great Wall was a bad idea.

Ⓒ The Great Wall was a Chinese folktale.

Her Name Was Sacajawea

In 1804, two men led an expedition to explore part of the West. Their names were Lewis and Clark. There were no maps, and they needed a guide. They hired a fur trader and his wife. Her name was Sacajawea (sah cuh juh WEE uh).

Sacajawea grew up in the Shoshone (shoh SHOH nee) tribe. She knew how to hunt and fish. She knew every inch of the land.

Sacajawea showed the men the best way to go. She found food when there was none. They walked through deep snow and paddled on rough waters. The journey was dangerous.

The trip was successful. Sacajawea is remembered as a brave woman who helped explore the West.

Sacajawea guided the Lewis and Clark expedition.

Fill in the letter with the best answer for each question.

1. From the article you can figure out that

   Ⓐ Sacajawea was Native American.

   Ⓑ Lewis and Clark were Native American.

   Ⓒ there were no Native Americans in the West.

2. If there were no maps, there also were probably no

   Ⓐ oceans.

   Ⓑ rivers.

   Ⓒ roads.

3. If Sacajawea had not gone on the journey,
   it might not have been

   Ⓐ dangerous.

   Ⓑ successful.

   Ⓒ fun.

4. Which statement do you think is true?

   Ⓐ Lewis and Clark were thankful to Sacajawea.

   Ⓑ Lewis and Clark were annoyed at Sacajawea.

   Ⓒ Sacajawea was a very old woman.

Rube Goldberg's Funny Pictures?

Rube Goldberg wanted to draw cartoons. His dad wanted him to be an engineer. Goldberg tried that first. Then he told his dad he just had to draw. So Goldberg worked as an office boy at a newspaper. He drew lots of cartoons for his boss. Finally, he got the job he wanted.

Goldberg knew there were two ways to do things—the simple way and the hard way. He believed people like doing things the hard way. So Goldberg's cartoons show very hard ways to do easy tasks.

Today people still laugh at Goldberg's cartoons. Look at this one. Does it make you laugh?

Fill in the letter with the best answer for each question.

1. Which statement is an opinion about Rube Goldberg?

   Ⓐ Rube Goldberg drew the funniest cartoons.

   Ⓑ Rube Goldberg worked as an office boy.

   Ⓒ Rube Goldberg was a cartoonist.

2. Which statement is a fact about Rube Goldberg?

   Ⓐ Everyone should laugh at Goldberg's cartoons.

   Ⓑ Goldberg's father should not have forced him
      to be an engineer.

   Ⓒ Goldberg's cartoons showed the hard way to do things.

3. How did Rube Goldberg get the job he wanted?

   Ⓐ He drew lots of cartoons for his boss.

   Ⓑ He became an engineer.

   Ⓒ He sold a book of cartoons.

4. Rube Goldberg became a cartoonist because

   Ⓐ he did things the hard way.

   Ⓑ his father was an engineer.

   Ⓒ he never gave up trying.

Titanic!

People said it was the safest ship ever built. It was the largest, for sure. How was it for the first-class passengers? No other ship could top its style. It had a big gym, tennis courts, and a huge swimming pool. There were elegant dining rooms

and ballrooms. They called it a "floating palace." It set sail for New York in 1912 with about 2,200 people on board.

Not long into the trip, the *Titanic* struck an iceberg. The "safest ship" began to sink. In that moment, the captain knew what would happen. Many people would die. Why? There were not enough lifeboats. The ship and its passengers sank to the bottom of the sea.

About 1,500 people died that night. How could something so awful, so terrible, happen? Why weren't there enough lifeboats? Some people say the builders took shortcuts. They wanted the ship to sail even though it wasn't ready.

In 1985, the wreck of the *Titanic* was found. Divers removed and brought up thousands of artifacts. These included jewelry and coins. Postcards and magazines were found, too. The wreckage told the real story. The ship had split in two and scattered pieces of people's lives all over the ocean floor. What was believed to be the safest ship is now famous for a very sad ending.

Fill in the letter with the best answer for each question.

1. The *Titanic* started to sink because it had

  Ⓐ sailed too fast.

  Ⓑ hit an iceberg.

  Ⓒ rained so hard.

  Ⓓ no lifeboats.

2. Because there were not enough lifeboats,

  Ⓐ people died.

  Ⓑ people swam for shore.

  Ⓒ people complained to the captain.

  Ⓓ people did nothing.

3. Because the wreck of the *Titanic* was found,

  Ⓐ workers are starting to rebuild the ship.

  Ⓑ thousands of artifacts have been brought up.

  Ⓒ we learned how much food was on board.

  Ⓓ traveling by ship is safer today.

4. The *Titanic* had been called a "floating palace" because it

  Ⓐ belonged to the king and queen.

  Ⓑ was very old.

  Ⓒ had a huge house on it.

  Ⓓ was big and elegant.

Video Games: Past and Present

In the 1930s, pinball machines were the closest thing to video games. These machines were very large. People had to go to restaurants and bowling alleys to play them.

In 1972, the video game Pong® was invented. It was a lot like Ping-Pong. People liked this new game. But this machine was big, too. Pong was played mostly in arcades.

That same year, a new game was made. This game could be put on home computers. People loved being able to play video games at home.

One of the first video-game characters was Pac-Man™. Pac-Man looked like a yellow smiling face. He chased little figures around the screen and then ate them!

Many other games followed Pac-Man. Today, video games have better graphics and sounds. You can even play some of them on your phone!

What do you think will be the next step in video games?

Fill in the letter with the best answer for each question.

1. In which group do video games belong?

   Ⓐ board games

   Ⓑ water games

   Ⓒ electronic games

   Ⓓ outdoor games

2. The game Pac-Man does not fit in the group of

   Ⓐ games with moving figures.

   Ⓑ games that look like Ping-Pong.

   Ⓒ games that are played on screens.

   Ⓓ games that are played indoors.

3. Why did people like Pong?

   Ⓐ They could press a button.

   Ⓑ They could play it at home.

   Ⓒ It was like football.

   Ⓓ It was like Ping-Pong.

4. Why do you think so many people play video games today?

   Ⓐ They have nothing else to do.

   Ⓑ They can play these games only at home.

   Ⓒ They can play these games almost anywhere.

   Ⓓ They don't like other kinds of games.

Raining Frogs?

What is odd about what Goran sees?

1   Winds blew dark clouds across
2 the sky. Goran, in bed with the flu,
3 watched from his window. He expected
4 heavy rain. But instead of water, he
5 saw tiny frogs falling!
6   Goran wondered if fever made him
7 see things. He called for his mother,
8 who hurried in. "Mama, can it rain
9 frogs?" he asked.
10   His mother touched his hot
11 forehead. "Your fever makes you dream
12 things. I will bring you cold water to help you feel better."
13   On her way to the kitchen, Mama stopped. She saw tiny
14 frogs hopping everywhere outside. They were crossing the
15 road, jumping on the porch, and leaping in her garden.
16 People were out looking at the frogs. Mama called, "Are
17 they real?"
18   "Yes!" one said. "This is a windstorm. Winds can spin
19 very fast, like a tornado. These winds probably passed over
20 ponds with baby frogs in them. The wind sucked up the
21 water and the frogs in it. When the wind calmed down,
22 everything fell from the sky. So we did have falling frogs!"
23   Mama returned to Goran's room. "Darling, your
24 forehead is warm but your eyes are clear. You did see frogs
25 falling like rain."

▶ **Answer each question. Give evidence from the mystery.**

1. Why is Goran in bed (line 2)?

Ⓐ He just woke up.   Ⓒ He wants to see frogs.

Ⓑ He doesn't feel well.   Ⓓ He likes to read in bed.

What helped you pick your answer? _____

_____

_____

2. Which best describes how a tornado moves?

Ⓐ It flashes.   Ⓑ It leaps.   Ⓒ It rumbles.   Ⓓ It twirls.

How did you pick your answer? _____

_____

_____

3. Why did Mama touch Goran's forehead (lines 10 and 11)?

_____

_____

4. Why is this story a mystery? Explain. _____

_____

_____

_____

Breaker Boy

How can you tell that Chet lived long ago?

1   Chet was eight years old. He told the boss he was 12
2   and small for his age. Everybody knew that was a lie. But
3   that lie got him a job as a breaker boy.
4   Chet woke up every day at five, ate a biscuit, and put
5   on his dusty clothes. He walked for an hour to get to the
6   mine. He had to be on his wood bench by seven. The
7   breaker room was as hot as an oven in summer. It was as
8   cold as an icebox in winter. The air was dirty all year long.
9   Chunks of coal mixed with other materials passed
10 below Chet's feet on a moving belt. He and the others
11 picked out anything that wasn't coal. It might be clumps
12 of clay, slabs of slate, or plain rocks. It was boring and
13 dangerous work. But it earned him money.
14   Chet's filthy hands were red with scrapes and cuts.
15 Gloves were not allowed. His back, neck, and arms were
16 sore from bending
17 all day. But what
18 choice was there? He,
19 Ma, and the babies
20 needed money. So no
21 more school for Chet.
22 No more farm work
23 either. Just long, hard
24 days of work.

Breaker boys at work

▶ **Answer each question. Give evidence from the story.**

1. What was the breaker room like in summer?

Ⓐ It was rocky and dark.   Ⓒ It was cool and calm.

Ⓑ It was way too hot.   Ⓓ It was warm and cozy.

What helped you pick your answer? _____

_____

_____

2. Why did Chet lie about his age?

Ⓐ He was too young for the job he needed.

Ⓑ He liked working with older boys.

Ⓒ He was ashamed he was so small.

Ⓓ He wanted to miss school.

How did you choose your answer?_____

_____

3. Explain the job of a breaker boy. _____

_____

_____

4. Look closely at the photo. Tell how it fits Chet's story. _____

_____

_____

The Golden Touch

Legend From Greece

What happens in the story to change King Midas?

1 Long ago there lived a rich man called
2 King Midas. He was richer than anyone
3 on Earth. Still, he always wanted more.
4 One day, a wizard granted King Midas
5 one wish. "May all that I touch turn to
6 gold!" At once, his wish came true.
7 King Midas loved his new power. He
8 spent all day touching things. He turned
9 flowers, trees, and rocks into gold. He
10 turned tables and chairs into gold. Midas
11 was giddy with golden delight.
12 That night, King Midas sat on his golden throne and
13 called for supper. He took a red apple. But before he could
14 bite into it, it turned to gold. He tried to eat some bread,
15 but it turned to gold. He drank from a gold goblet, but the
16 water in it turned to gold as it touched his lips. Midas went
17 to bed hungry.
18 The next day, the king's daughter came to him for her
19 morning hug. Before Midas realized what would happen,
20 his touch turned her into a gold statue. "NO MORE!" Midas
21 cried. "What use is gold without my sweet girl? I don't want
22 this golden touch anymore!"
23 The wizard appeared and turned everything gold back
24 into what it was before. King Midas hugged his daughter,
25 and the two shared a huge breakfast.

▶ **Answer each question. Give evidence from the legend.**

1. What made Midas want to end his golden touch?

Ⓐ It was hard turning things into gold.   Ⓒ He grew bored with gold.

Ⓑ He turned his daughter into a statue.   Ⓓ He couldn't eat or drink.

What helped you pick your answer? _____

_____

_____

2. When King Midas felt *giddy* (line 11), he felt _____.

Ⓐ joyful   Ⓑ bright   Ⓒ worried   Ⓓ ashamed

How did you pick your answer? _____

_____

_____

3. Why was Midas foolish to wish for a golden touch? _____

_____

_____

4. Why did King Midas have such a big breakfast (lines 23 and 24)?

_____

_____

_____

Unicorn Secrets

What makes this story a fantasy?

1   Do you believe in unicorns? Most people say that
2 unicorns aren't real, so you probably don't. But when my
3 grandmother was nine, she met a unicorn in the woods one
4 summer night. Both were scared and shy, but they became
5 friends. My grandmother learned these unicorn secrets,
6 which she shared with me.

7   • Swim every night in fresh cold water. This keeps your
8   horn and coat clean so they can shine in the moonlight.
9   • Sip goat's milk and dewdrops. These liquids give you
10   powerful legs and tough teeth.
11   • Eat fresh cobwebs every day. They help your mane and
12   tail to grow silky and strong.
13   • Run along a sandy beach or rocky trail every day.
14   Your hooves and your balance will become sturdy.
15   • Look deeply into someone's eyes to find his or her true
16   feelings. Eyes never lie.
17   • Pick your friends with
18   care. Choose only those
19   who will always be kind
20   and true.
21   As for me, I don't
22 believe in unicorns at
23 all. Still, I think that my
24 grandmother got some very
25 good advice somehow!

horn   mane   tail   coat   hooves

▶ **Answer each question. Give evidence from the fantasy.**

1. What do most people believe about unicorns?

Ⓐ Unicorns breathe fire.   Ⓒ Unicorns are not real.

Ⓑ Unicorns are friendly.   Ⓓ Unicorns are very smart.

What helped you pick your answer? _____

_____

2. What is the unicorn's secret for knowing if someone is telling the truth?

Ⓐ Swim every night in fresh cold water.

Ⓑ Sip goat's milk and dewdrops.

Ⓒ Talk to friends in the woods.

Ⓓ Look deeply into his or her eyes.

How did you pick your answer? _____

_____

3. In lines 7 and 8, the unicorn tells how to keep your *coat* clean.
What does the unicorn mean by *coat*?

_____

4. Which of the secrets make sense for people to follow? Explain.

_____

_____

_____

Word Wizard

What can you do when you read a word that has many meanings?

1 Suppose you are reading an interesting story.
2 Suddenly, you come to a word. You can read the word,
3 but the meanings you know for it just don't make sense.

4 Her albums were a **mine** of family history.

5 Lucky for you, there is a special book to help you. It is a
6 *dictionary*.
7 A dictionary gives a meaning for every word it lists.
8 Look up the word *mine*. Find the meaning that works
9 best in the sentence.

Entry word

How to say the word

10 **mine** (mine)

11 **1.** PRONOUN the one that belongs to me:
12 *This desk is mine.*

13 **2.** NOUN a large tunnel or space made in
14 the earth to dig out valuable things

15 **3.** NOUN a small bomb hidden underground
16 or underwater

Definitions with part of speech

17 **4.** VERB to dig minerals out of the ground:
18 *They mine silver down there.*

19 **5.** NOUN a rich supply:
20 *Dad is a mine of sports facts.*

▶ **Answer each question. Give evidence from the passage.**

1. How many different meanings of *mine* does this dictionary entry give?

Ⓐ one   Ⓑ three   Ⓒ five   Ⓓ seven

What helped you pick your answer? _____

_____

2. What does this dictionary entry NOT give?

Ⓐ other words that mean the same as *mine*

Ⓑ examples of sentences with *mine* in them

Ⓒ how to pronounce *mine*

Ⓓ how to spell *mine*

How did you pick your answer? _____

_____

3. Which meaning of *mine* fits the sentence in line 4? Explain.

_____

_____

4. Read this sentence: We visited an old copper *mine*.
Which meaning of *mine* best fits this sentence? Explain.

_____

_____

The ABCs of 9-1-1

How does this poster present information?

9-1-1

1 **What is 9-1-1?**
2 9-1-1 is a FREE phone
3 number to call in an
4 emergency. Call 9-1-1 for
5 FAST help for yourself or
6 someone else.

7 **When do I call 9-1-1?**
8 Dial 9-1-1 ONLY if a
9 person is hurt or in
10 danger. Dial for help
11 from the police, a doctor,
12 or a firefighter.

13 **Who answers?**
14 The person who answers
15 knows how to get you the
16 right kind of help. That
17 person will ask questions.
18 Your answers guide the
19 9-1-1 operator to the kind
20 of help you need most.

21 **Why must I answer**
22 **questions?**
23 The operator must know
24 who you are, where you
25 are, and what's wrong.
26 He or she will also tell
27 you what to do until help
28 gets there.

29 **How do I talk to the**
30 **operator?**
31 Stay calm. Speak clearly.
32 Describe the problem with
33 facts, such as your exact
34 address and full name.

35 **When is the call over?**
36 Stay on the phone until
37 you get the OK to hang up.
38 Even if you have nothing
39 more to say, let the operator
40 hear what's going on.

▶ **Answer each question. Give evidence from the poster.**

1. Which would also make a good title for this poster?

Ⓐ How to Make a Telephone Call   Ⓒ When You Have a Bad Cold

Ⓑ What to Do in an Emergency   Ⓓ Who Invented 9-1-1?

What helped you pick your answer? _____

_____

_____

2. Which is not an *emergency*?

Ⓐ A fire breaks out in the kitchen.

Ⓑ A person falls and is too hurt to get up.

Ⓒ There is a squirrel in the attic.

Ⓓ A worker gets badly cut by a saw.

How did you pick your answer?_____

_____

3. When should a 9-1-1 call end? _____

_____

4. Why is it important to stay calm and speak clearly when you call 9-1-1?

_____

_____

About an Illustrator

Why does the writer use Pinkney's own words?

1   Jerry Pinkney is a "storyteller
2 at heart." He has been a book
3 illustrator for more than 50
4 years. He has made the art for
5 more than 100 books. Many of
6 them have won awards.

Jerry Pinkney

7   Pinkney began drawing as
8 a young boy. He says, "At some
9 point I realized I'd rather sit and
10 draw than do almost anything
11 else." By first grade, he was the
12 class artist. He always had a
13 pad and pencil with him. When
14 he wasn't using them, he would
15 look for little details all around him.

16   But school wasn't easy for Pinkney. He didn't read
17 as well as other kids did. No matter how hard he tried,
18 he was a slow reader. He recalls, "I felt calm when I was
19 making pictures. When I was drawing, I knew that I was
20 using my mind."

21   Pinkney focuses hard when he draws. "I don't see
22 things until I draw them. When I put a line down, the
23 only thing I know is how it should feel. I know when it
24 doesn't feel right. I work with a pencil in one hand and
25 an eraser in the other." He believes that every mistake is
26 a new chance to do better.

▶ **Answer each question. Give evidence from the passage.**

1. Jerry Pinkney knew that he was using his mind when he was _____.

Ⓐ in first grade   Ⓒ making pictures

Ⓑ trying to read   Ⓓ carrying a pad and pencil

What helped you pick your answer? _____

_____

2. What job do illustrators do?

Ⓐ Illustrators erase things.   Ⓒ Illustrators write books.

Ⓑ Illustrators win awards.   Ⓓ Illustrators make pictures.

How did you pick your answer? _____

_____

_____

3. Explain why school was hard for young Jerry Pinkney.

_____

_____

4. Why doesn't Jerry Pinkney worry about making mistakes when he draws? Explain.

_____

_____

_____

Horse Sense

How does the title fit the essay?

1 Sayings can stand for something other than what
2 the words seem to mean. Such sayings are called
3 *idioms.* Suppose your dad says, "Hold your tongue!"
4 Does he want you to grab your tongue? No, he wants
5 you to stop talking.

6 English has many *horse* idioms. This may be
7 because so many people used to have or use horses.
8 Teachers might ask groups to *stop horsing around.* This
9 means to stop acting wild and noisy.

10 Did you ever get a bad leg cramp? A nurse might
11 call it a *Charley horse,* no matter what your name is!
12 Nobody knows for sure how this old idiom got started.

13 Can you trust a report that *comes straight from the*
14 *horse's mouth*? Usually you can. This idiom means
15 that the person who reported the event was there
16 when it happened.

17 *Don't put the cart*
18 *before the horse* is a
19 warning: Do things in
20 order. If you zip your
21 jacket before you put
22 it on, you put the cart
23 before the horse. Maybe
24 you do this because you
25 have no *horse sense*!

▶ **Answer each question. Give evidence from the essay.**

1. Which of the following is NOT an idiom?

Ⓐ Comes straight from the horse's mouth ⒸStop horsing around!

Ⓑ Feed hay to that hungry horse! Ⓓ Hold your tongue!

What helped you pick your answer? _____

_____

_____

2. Which shows *Don't put the cart before the horse*?

Ⓐ eating your cereal and then pouring milk in the bowl

Ⓑ opening the closet and then hanging up your coat

Ⓒ putting on your socks and then your shoes

Ⓓ washing the dishes and then drying them

How did you pick your answer? _____

_____

3. Explain what an idiom is. _____

_____

_____

4. What does it mean to have *horse sense* (title and line 25)? Explain.

_____

_____

What's in My Pocket?

What does Brian have in his pocket?
Fill in the blanks to find out.

One day, Brian asked his parents, "Can you

_____ what's in my pocket?"

His mom asked, "Is it pink like the nose of a kitten?

Or blue like your _____?"

Brian shook his head. His dad asked, "Is it soft like

a bunny's tail? Or hard like a _____

and pail?"

Brian shook his head. Dad asked, "Can it _____

or crawl? Can it roll like a ball?"

Brian laughed and said, "No! Give up?"

"Yes," they _____. "Just TELL us!"

Brian said, "It's not pink or blue. It's not soft or hard. It can't crawl

or roll . . . because it's a great big HOLE!"

Word List

- guess
- mittens
- nodded
- shovel
- wiggle

Think About It!   What can you tell about Brian from reading this story?

The Stars and Stripes

Read this poem to find out about the stars and stripes on our flag. Use the word list to fill in the blanks.

We live in the land of the free.

Our flag flies high for all to see.

Red, white, and blue are the colors we see.

The flag tells about our country's _____.

The story begins with thirteen stripes,

Seven are red, and six are white.

From one to fifty—now count each star.

That's how many states there are!

We fly the flag on _____ days.

We _____ the flag and give it _____.

Oh, say can you see, in this land of the free,

How _____ our flag flies for you and me?

Word List

praise
history
proudly
salute
special

Think About It!

What are some reasons people fly the U.S. flag?

Wild, Wild Snowstorm

Have you ever seen a blizzard? Fill in the blanks to find out about these wild storms.

A blizzard is a wild snowstorm. It snows for hours and hours. Sometimes, it snows for days! The air is _____ cold. Strong _____ of wind make trees sway and cause high _____. These mounds of snow can bury cars. It might take days, even weeks to _____ the cars.

Whiteouts are caused by _____ snow. That's when the sky and ground look like a big white sheet! It's easy to get lost in a whiteout.

Protect yourself and your pets during a blizzard. Stay inside until the snow stops. Then go out and have some fun!

Word List

drifts
gusts
freezing
swirling
uncover

Think About It!

What's the difference between a regular snowstorm and a blizzard?

Cat Chat

Can cats talk? Fill in the blanks to learn why the author says, "My cat tells me a lot."

My cat Pearl can't really talk, but she tells me a lot. She does so in her own way. Pearl certainly knows how to _____ her feelings. I just have to pay _____ to what she does.

Like all cats, Pearl says, "meow." One kind of meow is a friendly _____. It means, "Hello, I'm glad to see you."

A very loud meow is _____. It means, "Look at me! Something is wrong! I need help!"

Pearl's purr sounds like a motor. It tells me very clearly that she is happy. Pearl purrs softly when she smells food and when I pet her.

If Pearl rubs against my leg, I know she's saying, "I'm hungry!" When she rolls on her back and _____, she's saying, "I like you and trust you." My cat tells me a lot.

Word List

attention
communicate
different
greeting
stretches

Think About It!

What are some of the ways Pearl communicates?

A Visit From the Sea

Through the ages, people have told stories about the sun and the moon. Fill in the blanks as you read this story about how the sun and moon came to live in the sky.

Long ago, the Sun and the Moon were very good friends with the Sea. Every day Sun and Moon visited Sea. But Sea never visited the Sun and Moon, and that hurt their feelings.

Finally, they asked Sea why he never visited. "Your house is not big enough," said Sea. "I couldn't fit."

So Sun and Moon built a _____ house. It was so big that it took a whole day to walk across it. Surely Sea would fit.

The next day Sea visited. He _____ into the house until the water was waist high. "Should I stop?" he asked.

"No, no," said Sun and Moon. So Sea kept flowing. Soon, he reached the _____. Sun and Moon had to sit on the roof.

Finally, the whole house was _____, including the roof. Sun and Moon had to leap onto a cloud _____ by. And that's how Sun and Moon came to live in the sky.

Word List

- ceiling
- floating
- flowed
- huge
- underwater

Think About It!

What caused Sun and Moon to live in the sky?

My Favorite Dentist

Do you like to go to the dentist? Many kids don't...but fill in the blanks to read about one kid who does.

Some kids are scared to go to the dentist, but not me. I have a funny dentist named Dr. Smileyface. I don't think that's his real name, but that's what he tells the kids. He has a cool _____ room with _____ games and a big toy box. He asks goofy questions like, "Are you _____ yet?" and "Do you eat flowers to make your breath smell sweet?" One time he told me this joke. "What has lots of teeth, but never goes to the dentist? A _____!" When I laughed, he pulled my tooth. It didn't hurt at all. He also tells me to brush so I don't get a _____ the size of the Grand Canyon. When I leave, he sends me home with a _____. Last time, it was a rubber spider to scare my mom with. Now she's afraid of my trips to the dentist!

Word List

- cavity
- comb
- married
- surprise
- video
- waiting

Think About It!

Why do you think the dentist does such silly things?

It's Slinky® Time!

Have you ever wondered who made the first "Slinky"? Read this article to find out. Use the word list to fill in the blanks.

Have you ever played with a Slinky toy? It looks like a snake, but it's made from thin wire or plastic. Stretch it out, then let it go. It can "walk" down stairs!

Richard James _____ the Slinky toy in 1943. He _____ a gigantic spring fall off a shelf. It rolled over a table and _____ to the floor. James thought it could be an _____ toy. It took several years to get it right. Then he sold 400 in one day! Next, James made a _____ to coil the wire. Millions of Slinky toys have been sold since.

Word List

amusing

invented

machine

tumbled

watched

Think About It!

What gave Richard James the idea for the Slinky?

Oh, No!

How do rumors get started? Fill in the blanks to find out how one rumor was spread.

One day a hare was sleeping _____ a tree. Then something fell down with a loud THUD! The ground shook. The hare jumped up and started running. He shouted, "Oh, no! The earth is breaking apart!"

A deer spotted him and asked, "What's the matter?"

"The earth is breaking apart!" said the _____ hare. The deer followed the hare. They ran past a rhinoceros.

"The earth is breaking apart!" they shouted. The rhino joined them.

A lion heard the animals _____ by. "What's the matter?" he asked. They told him that the earth was breaking apart. "The earth seems quite _____ to me. Just how did this tale get started?" the lion asked.

The hare explained and said, "Follow me."

When they reached the tree, something fell to the earth with a THUD! The lion _____. "You heard this coconut hitting the ground. Don't listen to rumors!"

Word List
beneath
laughed
solid
terrified
thundering

Think About It! Why did the hare think the earth was breaking apart?

88

Here Comes the Parade!

Every Thanksgiving there is a big parade in New York City. Fill in the blanks to find out all about it.

Thanksgiving is a busy day. The night before is busy, too, at least in New York City. Macy's workers pump up _____ balloons! They are for the Macy's Thanksgiving Day Parade. In the morning, people will crowd the streets. _____ will watch it on TV.

Word List

directors
giant
helium
millions
volunteers

There are dozens of balloons. Some of them are ten stories high! They are filled with air. The air is mixed with a gas called _____. This gas makes them float high in the air. _____ walk down the street and hold the balloons down with ropes.

Here's Kermit! There's Buzz Lightyear! Look at Shrek, over there! The big balloons look alive. They look out with their big eyes.

Every year, there are new balloons. Thousands of kids write letters to the _____ who plan the parade. They ask for new balloons. The parade planners try to use their ideas. Maybe you could come up with an idea for next year's parade!

Think About It!

What happens at the Macy's Thanksgiving Day Parade?

Art From Junk

What did one artist do with a pile of junk? Read this article to find out. Then fill in the blanks using words from the word list.

Alexander Calder's father was a sculptor. His mother was a painter. He became an artist, too.

As a child, Calder loved to save scraps. He collected pieces of string, wire, and cans. Calder used these pieces to make toys and _____.

As an _____, Calder used scraps to make sculptures. Sculptures are statues or figures. They can be made from all kinds of things. Calder used his "junk" to make art.

What kind of art can you _____ out of junk? Calder made a bird out of cans. He made a tiny dog using a _____ for its head. He made sculptures using metal scraps. Some had parts that moved. They were called _____. Calder was famous for his scrap metal art. Like both his parents, Calder worked hard at making art that others would enjoy.

Word List

adult
clothespin
construct
gadgets
mobiles

Think About It!

What words would you use to describe Calder?

Home, Sweet Home!

How do ants and termites build their homes? Fill in the blanks to find out.

Tiny insects build the most _____ homes. They build them to protect themselves and their families.

Ants build _____ mazes of tunnels and rooms. There are _____ for eggs, places to store food, and rooms for sleeping. They are always working on their homes. New tunnels are built. Walls are _____. The ants work so hard that they need to sleep all winter!

Termites build castles. They make tiny holes on the outside to create an air-conditioning _____!

Some termite mounds are shaped like mushrooms. Others are shaped like barrels. And some are as tall as giraffes.

Termites make mud using dirt and spit. Then they use this mud to build homes with very strong, thick walls. Farmers sometimes have to clear termite nests from their fields. Some towers are so strong that the only way to shatter them is to blow them up with _____!

Word List

amazing
chambers
dynamite
system
underground
repaired

Think About It!

How are ant and termite homes alike? How are they different?

Handwriting

Name

Tip: Look at the arrows to see how to form each letter.

A B C D E F G H I J K L M
N O P Q R S T U V W X Y Z

Use your best handwriting to copy each letter below.

Ha! • Ha! • Ha! • Ha! • Ha! • Ha! • Ha! • Ha!

Bonus Chuckle!

What do you call a crying camel?

A humpback wail!

Name _____

manuscript handwriting

Tip: Look at the arrows to see how to form each letter.

a b c d e f g h i j k l m n
o p q r s t u v w x y z

Use your best handwriting to copy each letter below.

Ha! · Ha! · Ha! · Ha! · Ha! · Ha!

Name _____

Name _____

Use your best handwriting to copy the words.

do   porcupine   turtle

Use your best handwriting to copy the sentences below.

What do you get when you cross a porcupine with a turtle?

A real slowpoke!

Ha! • Ha! • Ha! • Ha! • Ha! • Ha! • Ha! • Ha!

Tip: Begin letters from the top, not the bottom.

Bonus Chuckle!

How do turtles communicate with other turtles?

Shell phones!

Name

Use your best handwriting to copy the words.

butterfly

to   was

Tip: Pull the pencil toward the middle of your body when you write.

Use your best handwriting to copy the sentences below.

Why wasn't the butterfly invited to the dance?

Because the dance was a moth-ball!

Ha! • Ha! • Ha! • Ha! • Ha! • Ha! • Ha!

MOTH BALL

Bonus Chuckle!

Why did the little boy throw butter out the window?

He wanted to see the butter fly!

95

Name _____

Use your best handwriting to copy the words.

Use your best handwriting to copy the sentences below.

What is harder than getting a rhino into a phone booth?

Getting two rhinos into a phone booth!

Ha! • Ha! • Ha! • Ha! • Ha! • Ha! • Ha! • Ha!

Tip: Use your pinkie finger or a paper clip to measure the space between each word.

Bonus Chuckle!

What should you do if you see a blue rhino?

Cheer it up!

Copyright © Scholastic Inc.

96

Name ____________________

Use your best handwriting to copy the words.

girl oil mouse

Use your best handwriting to copy the sentences below.

Why did the little girl pour oil on her new pet mouse?
Because it was squeaking!

Tip: All uppercase letters should touch the top and bottom lines.

Ha! Ha! Ha! Ha! Ha! Ha! Ha! Ha! Ha!

Bonus Chuckle!

What game does every mouse love to play?

Hide and squeak!

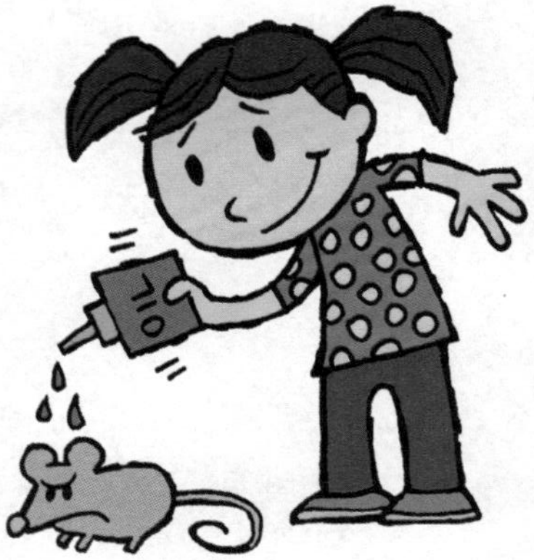

Name _____

Use your best handwriting to copy the words.

mosquito   go   bite

Use your best handwriting to copy the sentences below.

Why did the mosquito go to see the dentist?

He wanted to improve his bite!

Tip:
Lowercase letters *b, d, f, h,* and *l* are tall. They all touch the top line.

Ha! • Ha! • Ha! • Ha! • Ha! • Ha! • Ha! • Ha!

Bonus Chuckle!

What do you get when you cross a mosquito and a snowman?

Frostbite!

Name

Use your best handwriting to copy the words.

pig

home

school

Use your best handwriting to copy the sentences below.

Why did the little pig go straight home after school?

He had lots and lots of ham-work to do!

Ha! • Ha! • Ha! • Ha! • Ha! • Ha!

Bonus Chuckle!

Where did the pioneer keep his pigs?

In a hog cabin!

Copyright © Scholastic Inc.

Tip: Lowercase letters *g, p, q,* and *y* have tails. The tails hang down below the bottom line.

Name _____

Use your best handwriting to copy the words.

chicken　　　　get　　　　slide

_____

_____

Use your best handwriting to copy the sentences below.

Why did the chicken cross the playground?

He wanted to get to the other slide!

Ha! · Ha! · Ha! · Ha! · Ha! · Ha! · Ha! · Ha!

_____

_____

_____

_____

_____

_____

_____

Tip: Try to make all of your letters stand up straight.

Bonus Chuckle!

What do you call a funny book for chickens?

A yolk book!

100

Name

Use your best handwriting to copy the words.

ant   great   uncle

Use your best handwriting to copy the sentences below.

What do you call an ant that lives with your great uncle? Your great ant, of course!

Ha! • Ha! • Ha! • Ha! • Ha! • Ha!

Tip: Always take your time when practicing your handwriting.

101

Name _____

Use your best handwriting to copy the words.

worm   apple   half

Use your best handwriting to copy the sentences below.

What is the only thing worse than finding a worm
in your apple? Finding half a worm in your apple!

Ha! • Ha! • Ha! • Ha! • Ha! • Ha! • Ha! • Ha!

_____

_____

_____

_____

Tip: If you are coming to the end of the line, begin the next word on the following line.

Bonus Chuckle!

How can you tell which end of a worm is **which?**

Tickle both and see which one laughs!

Name _____

manuscript handwriting

Use your best handwriting to copy the words.

rabbit   whole   wide

Use your best handwriting to copy the sentences below.

Who is the strongest rabbit in the whole wide world?

Hare-cules!

Ha! • Ha! • Ha! • Ha! • Ha! • Ha!

Bonus Chuckle!

What is a rabbit's favorite dance style?

Hip-hop!

Name _____

Use your best handwriting to copy the words.

fly   between   bird

Use your best handwriting to copy the sentences below.

What is the difference between a fly and a bird?

A bird can fly but a fly cannot bird!

Ha! • Ha! • Ha! • Ha! • Ha! • Ha! • Ha! • Ha! • Ha!

Tip: You can practice writing your letters in the sand.

Bonus Chuckle!

Why did the fly fly?

Because the spider spied 'er!

104

Name _____

manuscript handwriting

Use your best handwriting to copy the words.

owl

voice

hoot

Tip: You can practice writing your letters on your friend's back.

Use your best handwriting to copy the sentences below.

What happened when the owl lost his voice?

Nothing, because he did not give a hoot!

Ha! • Ha! • Ha! • Ha! • Ha! • Ha!

*

Bonus Chuckle!

What is green and loves to peck at trees?

Woody Wood-pickle!

Name _____

Use your best handwriting to copy the words.

turkey   prove   not

Use your best handwriting to copy the sentences below.

Why did the turkey decide to skydive?

He had to prove that he was not chicken!

Ha! • Ha! • Ha! • Ha! • Ha! • Ha! • Ha!

Tip: You can practice writing your letters with finger paints.

Bonus Chuckle!

What is a turkey's favorite dessert?

Peach gobbler!

106

Name

Use your best handwriting to copy the words.

snakes   funny   joke

Use your best handwriting to copy the sentences below.

What do snakes say when they hear a very funny joke?

"That was so hiss-terical!"

HA! HA! HA! HA!

Ha! • Ha! • Ha! • Ha! • Ha! • Ha!

Tip: Drawing circles, squares, and triangles will help you write better letters.

Bonus Chuckle!

What is a snake's favorite subject in school?

Hiss-story!

107

Name _____

Use your best handwriting to copy the words.

leopard   in   long

Use your best handwriting to copy the sentences below.

Did you hear what happened to the leopard who
stayed in the shower too long?   He became spotless!

Ha! · Ha! · Ha! · Ha! · Ha! · Ha! · Ha! · Ha!

Tip: Practice
your handwriting
a little each day.

**Bonus
Chuckle!**

What is the
difference
between a tiger
and a lion?

A tiger has the mane
part missing!

Name _____

Use your best handwriting to copy the words.

giraffe   for   school

Use your best handwriting to copy the sentences below.

Why was the little giraffe late for school?

Because his mom got stuck in a huge giraffic jam!

HONK! HONK!

Ha! • Ha! • Ha! • Ha! • Ha! • Ha! • Ha!

_ _ _ _ _ _ _ _ _ _ _ _ _ _ _ _

_ _ _ _ _ _ _ _ _ _ _ _ _ _ _ _

_ _ _ _ _ _ _ _ _ _ _ _ _ _ _ _

_ _ _ _ _ _ _ _ _ _ _ _ _ _ _ _

Tip: Make sure your pencil is nice and sharp before you begin writing.

109

Name _____

Use your best handwriting to copy the words.

kangaroo   to   see

Use your best handwriting to copy the sentences below.

Why did the kangaroo hop over to see his doctor?

He was feeling quite jumpy!

Ha! • Ha! • Ha! • Ha! • Ha! • Ha! • Ha! • Ha! • Ha! • Ha!

Tip: Make sure you have a good eraser before you begin writing.

DR. WOMBAT

Bonus Chuckle!

What is a kangaroo's favorite season?

Spring!

110

manuscript handwriting

Name _____

Use your best handwriting to copy the words.

little

say

penguin

Use your best handwriting to copy the sentences below.

What did the ocean say to the little penguin?

Nothing. It just waved!

Ha! • Ha! • Ha! • Ha! • Ha! • Ha!

Bonus Chuckle!

What is a penguin's favorite drink?

A waddle bottle!

Copyright © Scholastic Inc.

Tip: A clean desktop is the best place to practice your handwriting.

Name _____

Use your best handwriting to copy the words.

spider   did   crawl

_____   _____   _____

Use your best handwriting to copy the sentences below.

Why did the spider crawl across the computer
keyboard? He wanted to make a website!

Ha! · Ha! · Ha! · Ha! · Ha! · Ha! · Ha! · Ha!

_____

_____

_____

_____

_____

_____

manuscript handwriting

Tip: Always
try your very
best.

**Bonus
Chuckle!**

**Why did the
spider buy
a car?**

He wanted to go
for a spin!

Copyright © Scholastic Inc.

112

manuscript handwriting

Name _____

Use your best handwriting to copy the words.

grizzly

bear

rain

Use your best handwriting to copy the sentences below.

What do you call a grizzly bear that gets caught in the rain?

A drizzly bear!

Tip: Have a good time! Handwriting is fun.

Ha! • Ha! • Ha! • Ha! • Ha! • Ha!

Bonus Chuckle!

What is a polar bear's very favorite food?

A brrr-grrr!

Copyright © Scholastic Inc.

113

Name _____

Use your best cursive writing to copy each letter below.

$\mathcal{A}$ $\mathcal{B}$ $\mathcal{C}$ $\mathcal{D}$ $\mathcal{E}$ $\mathcal{F}$ $\mathcal{G}$ $\mathcal{H}$ $\mathcal{I}$ $\mathcal{J}$ $\mathcal{K}$ $\mathcal{L}$ $\mathcal{M}$

$\mathcal{N}$ $\mathcal{O}$ $\mathcal{P}$ $\mathcal{Q}$ $\mathcal{R}$ $\mathcal{S}$ $\mathcal{T}$ $\mathcal{U}$ $\mathcal{V}$ $\mathcal{W}$ $\mathcal{X}$ $\mathcal{Y}$ $\mathcal{Z}$

Tip: Use the arrows to guide you in forming each letter.

Bonus Chuckle!

What's an eight-letter word that has only one letter in it?

An envelope!

114

Name _____

cursive handwriting

a b c d e f g h i j k l m

n o p q r s t u v w x y z

Use your best cursive writing to copy each letter below.

Tip: Use the arrows to guide you in forming each letter.

Name _____

Use your best cursive writing to copy the words.

boy

homework

teacher

Use your best cursive writing to copy the sentences below.

Why did the boy eat up all of his homework?

Because his teacher said it was a piece of cake!

Ha! • Ha! • Ha! • Ha! • Ha! • Ha! • Ha! • Ha! • Ha!

Tip: Check your SIZE. Is each of your letters the right height and resting neatly on the line?

Bonus Chuckle!

What school supply is always sleepy?

A nap-sack!

Name _____

Use your best cursive writing to copy the words.

Cinderella

soccer

pumpkin

Use your best cursive writing to copy the sentences below.

Why did Cinderella lose every single soccer game? Because her coach was just a pumpkin!

Ha! • Ha! • Ha! • Ha! • Ha! • Ha! • Ha! • Ha!

Tip: Check your SLANT. Do all your letters slant in the same direction?

Bonus Chuckle!

What did Cinderella say when her photos didn't arrive?

"Someday my prints will come!"

Name _____

Use your best cursive writing to copy the words.

cat _____

yarn _____

mittens _____

Use your best cursive writing to copy the sentences below.

Did you hear what happened to the female cat that ate a big ball of yarn? She had a litter of mittens!

Ha! • Ha! • Ha! • Ha! • Ha! • Ha! • Ha! • Ha!

Tip: For extra practice copy your favorite quotes in cursive.

Bonus Chuckle!

Why are cats good at video games?

Because they have nine lives!

cursive handwriting

Name _____

Use your best cursive writing to copy the words.

President

standing

Because

Use your best cursive writing to copy the sentences below.

Why did President George Washington always sleep standing up? Because he could never lie!

Tip: Check your SHAPE. Are all of your letters the right shape and closed where they should be?

Ha! • Ha! • Ha! • Ha! • Ha! • Ha! • Ha!

Bonus Chuckle!

What do you call a gorilla in a top hat?

Ape-aham Lincoln!

Name _____

Use your best cursive writing to copy the words.

bacon

toast

egg

Use your best cursive writing to copy the sentences below.

Why did the bacon and toast begin to laugh?

Because the egg cracked an excellent yolk!

Ha! • Ha! • Ha! • Ha! • Ha! • Ha! • Ha! • Ha!

Tip: If you have to break a word at the end of the line, use a hyphen.

Bonus Chuckle!

What do you call cheese that does **not belong to you?**

Nacho cheese!

cursive handwriting

Name _____

Use your best cursive writing to copy the words.

teddy

bear

cake

Use your best cursive writing to copy the sentences below.

What did the teddy bear say when he was offered a

slice of cake? "No, thank you. I'm totally stuffed!"

Tip: Check your SHAPE. Are all of your letters the right shape and closed where they should be?

Ha! • Ha! • Ha! • Ha! • Ha! • Ha! • Ha! • Ha!

121

Name _____

Use your best cursive writing to copy the words.

lady

change

weather

Use your best cursive writing to copy the sentences below.

Why did the lady stand outside with her purse open?

She wanted to see if there was any change in the weather!

Ha! • Ha! • Ha! • Ha! • Ha! • Ha! • Ha! • Ha! • Ha! • Ha!

Tip:
Check your
SMOOTHNESS.
Do all of your
letters have
the same line
thickness?

Bonus Chuckle!

Why did the lady put lipstick on her forehead?

She need to make up her mind!

122

Name _____

Use your best cursive writing to copy the words.

flamingos

stand

would

Use your best cursive writing to copy the sentences below.

Why do flamingos lift one leg when they stand?
If they lifted both legs, they would fall down!

Ha! • Ha! • Ha! • Ha! • Ha! • Ha!

Tip: Clear your desk so you have room to write.

Where does a peacock go if it loses its tail?

A re-tail store!

123

Practice your handwriting here.

Grammar & Writing

Label each picture. Write a word on the line.

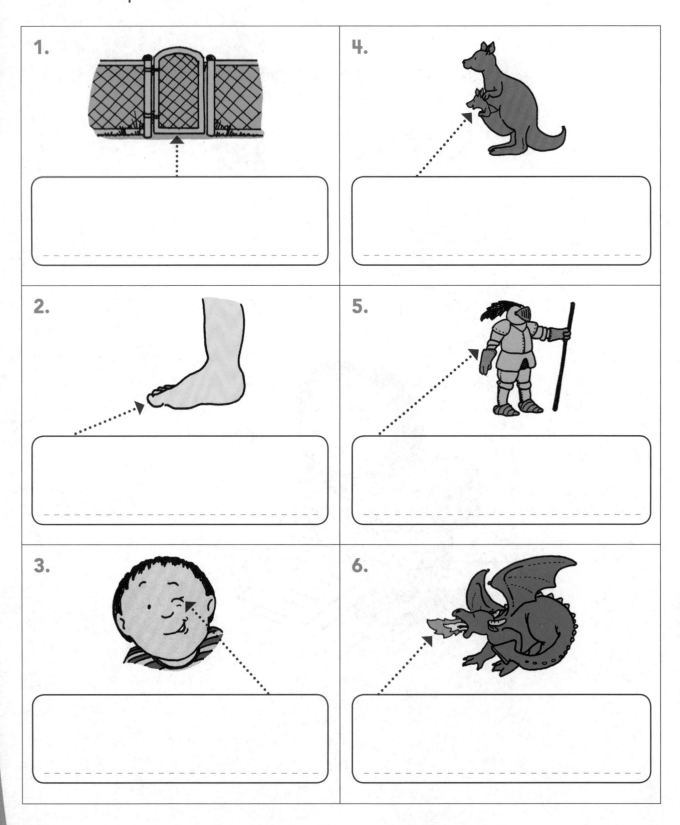

1.

2.

3.

4.

5.

6.

Label each picture. Write a word on the line.

1.

2.

3.

4.

5.

6.

Use all the words in each box to write a sentence. Remember to capitalize the first word and use ending punctuation.

1.
| old |
| the |
| is |
| cat |

_____

_____

_____

2.
| my |
| where |
| are |
| slippers |

_____

_____

_____

3.
| bake |
| some |
| cookies |
| let's |

_____

_____

_____

4.
| is |
| book |
| this |
| hard |
| too |

_____

_____

_____

5.
| right |
| who |
| answer |
| the |
| knows |

_____

_____

_____

Mark the letter of the word that is a noun.

> A **noun** is a word that names a person, place, thing, or idea.

1. That purple coat has shiny buttons.
   Ⓐ   Ⓑ   Ⓒ   Ⓓ

2. Why do clouds get so puffy?
   Ⓐ   Ⓑ   Ⓒ   Ⓓ

3. Actually, my best friend is younger than I am.
   Ⓐ   Ⓑ   Ⓒ   Ⓓ

4. All kids bring their lunches to school on Field Day.
   Ⓐ   Ⓑ   Ⓒ   Ⓓ

5. She bought a colorful postcard of Maine.
      Ⓐ   Ⓑ   Ⓒ   Ⓓ

6. Henry is the fastest runner in our class.
   Ⓐ   Ⓑ   Ⓒ   Ⓓ

7. Do you know where we can find blue polish?
   Ⓐ   Ⓑ   Ⓒ   Ⓓ

8. Long ago, pencils did not have erasers on them.
   Ⓐ   Ⓑ   Ⓒ   Ⓓ

9. If you ask me, that movie was boring.
   Ⓐ   Ⓑ   Ⓒ   Ⓓ

10. Neither of us has read that booklet.
    Ⓐ   Ⓑ   Ⓒ   Ⓓ

Each sentence has a noun shown in **boldface**. Write whether that noun names a **person**, a **place**, a **thing**, or an **idea**.

1. The giant **panda** is a kind of bear. _____

2. Pandas live in the forests of **China**. _____

3. **Scientists** thought they were related to raccoons. _____

4. Pandas can't roar, but they make a bleating **sound**. _____

5. Have you read *Giant Panda* by **Gail** Gibbons? _____

6. Pandas are popular with **visitors** to the zoo. _____

7. The zoo shop sells a cute panda **puppet**. _____

8. Zoo pandas don't have **freedom** to roam. _____

9. Pandas walk on all four **legs**. _____

10. Pandas spend most of their **time** eating. _____

11. Ruth **Harkness** brought the first live giant
    panda from China to America in 1936. _____

12. Capturing pandas is now against the **law**
    in China. _____

Nouns are naming words. **Precise nouns** name more exactly. Use better naming words to make your writing more clear.

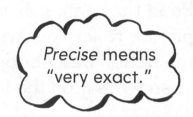

Precise means "very exact."

    Okay: My <u>pet</u> likes carrots.

    Better: My <u>gerbil</u> likes carrots.

Make each sentence better. Look in the big pencil for a better noun. Rewrite the sentence using that more precise noun.

1. I ate a spicy <u>food</u>.

_____

2. The <u>bird</u> flew so high.

_____

3. That old <u>toy</u> lost its tail.

_____

4. You need a <u>tool</u> to fix it.

_____

5. She likes the book's red <u>cover</u>.

_____

6. Let's make a play <u>place</u>.

_____

bear

castle

eagle

flute

hammer

jacket

kite

pepper

Read the sentences below. Look at the picture to find out who or what is doing the action described in the sentence. Then write it on the line.

The **subject** of a sentence tells who or what did something.

1. A _____ sits in the wagon.

2. A _____ rides in the wagon too.

3. _____ is pulling the wagon.

4. Her _____ wants a ride too.

5. The _____ can carry all the animals.

6. The _____ fly along with them.

Choose a word from the tent to use
as the subject of each sentence.

The subject of a sentence
is usually a noun.

shoes   clown

music   car

children   band

1. The _____ sit on the benches in the tent.

2. A small _____ drives into the ring.

3. This funny _____ jumps out.

4. His big _____ flop.

5. The _____ strikes up a tune.

6. Lively _____ fills the tent.

134

Study the picture. Read the words.
Write the plural of the word if there
is more than one in the picture.

Add **-s** to form the
plural of most nouns.

One	More than One	One	More than One
1. girl	_____	**7.** ball	_____
2. boy	_____	**8.** hoop	_____
3. doll	_____	**9.** man	_____
4. lion	_____	**10.** cap	_____
5. poster	_____	**11.** shirt	_____
6. balloon	_____	**12.** hand	_____

Mindy and Mandy always try to outdo each other. If Mindy has one peach, Mandy has two. If Mandy buys one shirt, Mindy buys two. Finish this talk between Mindy and Mandy. Write the plural for each word.

> Add **-es** to form the plural of nouns that end in *-sh, -ch, -x, -s,* or *-ss.*

1. **Mindy:** I have a new dress.

   Mandy: I have many new _____ .

2. **Mandy:** I will make a sandwich.

   Mindy: I will make two _____ .

3. **Mindy:** I saw a red fox.

   Mandy: I saw four red _____ .

4. **Mandy:** I bought this dish.

   Mindy: I bought these _____ .

5. **Mindy:** I took one bus.

   Mandy: I took three _____ .

6. **Mandy:** I will make a guess.

   Mindy: I will make a few _____ .

7. **Mindy:** I need one brush.

   Mandy: I need several _____ .

8. **Mandy:** I went to the beach.

   Mindy: I went to two _____ .

9. **Mindy:** I have a box.

   Mandy: I have five _____ .

10. **Mandy:** I planted a bush.

    Mindy: I planted two _____ .

The nouns in these sentences need a rest. Pick a pronoun to replace the underlined word(s). Then write the sentence with the pronoun.

> A **pronoun** is a word that can take the place of a noun.

Pronoun Subs					
he	you	we	they	it	she

1. <u>Tanya</u> swings the bat.

_____

2. <u>Mr. Bartlet and Mr. Jones</u> blow their whistles.

_____

3. <u>Matt and I</u> warm up.

_____

4. <u>Leo</u> looks for his glove.

_____

5. <u>The ball</u> rolls into the field.

_____

Circle the letter beside the pronoun that best completes the sentence.

1. Dad didn't bother to hang up _____ jacket.
   a. he   **b.** him   **c.** his   **d.** her

2. _____ just tossed the jacket onto the couch.
   a. He   **b.** Him   **c.** His   **d.** They

3. Queenie, our dog, needed a place
   to hide _____ bone.
   a. she   **b.** him   **c.** your   **d.** her

4. So _____ pushed it into the sleeve of the jacket.
   a. she   **b.** him   **c.** your   **d.** her

5. Dad remembered that _____ left a note in the jacket pocket.
   a. she   **b.** me   **c.** he   **d.** them

6. "Relax, dear. I'll get it for _____," said Mom.
   a. your   **b.** you   **c.** I   **d.** he

7. When she picked up the jacket, _____ felt too heavy.
   a. they   **b.** it   **c.** he   **d.** you

8. Something went *thud*, and Queenie ran in to see _____.
   a. him   **b.** them   **c.** it   **d.** I

9. "Well, Queenie," scolded Mom, "_____ are a rascal!"
   a. he   **b.** they   **c.** it   **d.** you

10. After that, _____ all had a good laugh together.
   a. we   **b.** us   **c.** them   **d.** my

Look at the different kinds of lists shown below. Pick one and check it off. Then write 10 things to do for that list. When you are finished, circle the verbs on your list.

> A **verb** is a word that tells what someone or something does. Most verbs show action.

❑ things to do after supper
❑ things to do with a friend
❑ things to do for a pet
❑ things to do in the snow
❑ things to do during summer
❑ things to do in school
❑ things to do in the park
❑ things to do on a rainy day

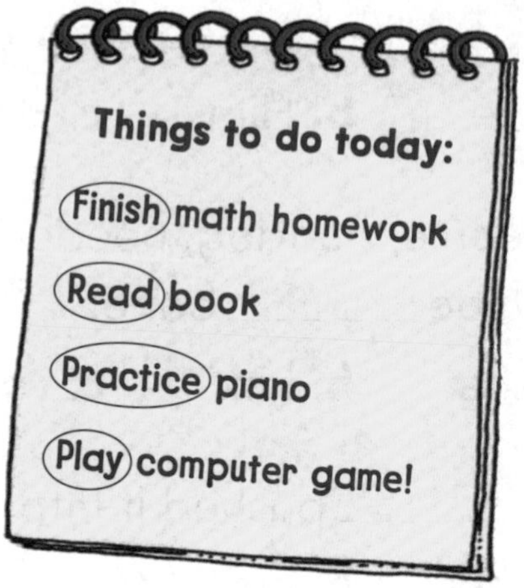

Things to do today:
(Finish) math homework
(Read) book
(Practice) piano
(Play) computer game!

1. _____
2. _____
3. _____
4. _____
5. _____
6. _____
7. _____
8. _____
9. _____
10. _____

Mark the letter of the word that is a verb.

1. <u>Many</u> <u>kinds</u> of animals <u>live</u> in the <u>rain forest</u>.
  Ⓐ Ⓑ   Ⓒ   Ⓓ

2. <u>Some</u> people <u>use</u> the word <u>jungle</u> <u>instead</u> of rain forest.
  Ⓐ   Ⓑ   Ⓒ Ⓓ

3. <u>Colorful</u> birds, such as <u>parrots</u>, <u>fly</u> through the <u>treetops</u>.
  Ⓐ   Ⓑ Ⓒ   Ⓓ

4. <u>Howler</u> <u>monkeys</u> <u>screech</u> at each <u>other</u> as they climb.
  Ⓐ   Ⓑ   Ⓒ   Ⓓ

5. Snakes <u>wrap</u> around <u>branches</u> <u>and</u> slither on the <u>ground</u>.
    Ⓐ   Ⓑ Ⓒ   Ⓓ

6. <u>You</u> can <u>hear</u> the <u>steady</u> hum of <u>insects</u> at work.
  Ⓐ   Ⓑ   Ⓒ   Ⓓ

7. Millions of creatures <u>make</u> <u>their</u> <u>homes</u> <u>in</u> rain forests.
         Ⓐ Ⓑ Ⓒ Ⓓ

8. <u>One</u> rain-forest <u>butterfly</u> <u>has</u> a wingspan <u>that</u> is a foot wide!
  Ⓐ   Ⓑ   Ⓒ   Ⓓ

9. Many <u>kinds</u> of plants <u>grow</u> <u>only</u> in <u>rain forests</u>.
   Ⓐ   Ⓑ Ⓒ   Ⓓ

10. <u>Scientists</u> <u>know</u> <u>of</u> <u>thousands</u> of kinds of ferns!
   Ⓐ   Ⓑ Ⓒ Ⓓ

140

verbs

In the sentences below, underline each action verb. Then draw a picture that shows the action. Be sure to show if it is one person or animal doing the action or more than one person or animal doing the action.

> Verbs tell when action takes place. **Present-tense verbs** tell about action that is happening now. A verb showing the action of one person ends in *-s*. A verb telling the action of more than one person does not end in *-s*. For example:
>
> The boy sings.   The boys sing.

1. Four birds sit on the fence.

2. That dog digs.

3. A man sells hotdogs.

4. The girls run.

Verbs express action. **Vivid verbs** express action so you can really picture it.

Good: *The duck <u>moves</u> to the water.*
Better: *The duck <u>waddles</u> to the water.*

Vivid means "lively, clear, or sharp."

Under each picture is a short sentence with a plain verb. Replace each plain verb with a vivid verb. Express the action more clearly.

A horse runs.

1. _____

A cat moves.

2. _____

A child plays.

3. _____

A bell sounds.

4. _____

A dog eats.

5. _____

A girl sees.

6. _____

Music plays.

7. _____

A child draws.

8. _____

A snake goes.

9. _____

The verbs in this story make no sense. Circle the verbs. Then rewrite the story with verbs that make sense. You should find 10 verbs.

> Alice lost the bread in the kitchen. She boiled the bread. Then she sprinkled jam on it. Alice chewed some juice too.
>
> The schoolbus disappeared at the corner.
>
> "Alice, you will push the bus!"
>
> So Alice quickly dropped her coat. She opened her books into her knapsack and waited out the door.
>
> "Here I reach!"

_____

_____

_____

_____

_____

_____

_____

_____

_____

Complete the chart. Add **-s**, **-ed**, and **-ing** to each base word.

Base Word	-s	-ed	-ing
cook			
test			
act			
order			
paint			

Complete the chart. Add **-s**, **-ed**, and **-ing** to each base word. Drop silent *e* when needed.

Base Word	-s	-ed	-ing
raise			
smile			
describe			
erase			
wiggle			

Circle the letter beside the verb form that best completes the sentence.

1. Joe and I decided to _____ the swimming team.
   a. join   **b.** joining   **c.** joins

2. We _____ swim classes three times a week.
   a. takes   **b.** take   **c.** taking

3. Our swim coach _____ a medal in the Olympics.
   a. winned   **b.** won   **c.** win

4. She _____ us practice over and over.
   a. makes   **b.** make   **c.** maked

5. Last week, we _____ the butterfly stroke.
   a. learn   **b.** learned   **c.** learns

6. I think it _____ the hardest stroke to do.
   a. be   **b.** is   **c.** are

7. But I love to make the water _____ as I go.
   a. splash   **b.** splashes   **c.** splashed

8. Last time, I _____ too much water in my nose.
   a. get   **b.** gets   **c.** got

9. It _____ me cough and sneeze, but I got over it.
   a. make   **b.** made   **c.** making

10. Can you _____ to our swim meet next week?
    a. coming   **b.** came   **c.** come

Write a form of the verb shown in **boldface** to finish each sentence. The first one has been done for you.

1. Yesterday I **ate** tuna for lunch, but today I will _____eat_____ pizza.

2. At her party last year, Jenny **blew** out only three candles.

This year, she will _____ out all of them!

3. Today Jed **drinks** lemonade with his lunch, but yesterday

he _____ milk.

4. Can you **dig** a hole as deep as the one we _____

over there?

5. Paco **brings** the snack for today because Ramon

_____ the snack last time.

6. Ed **forgot** the words to the song, but I won't _____ them.

7. Lori **left** at five, but we won't _____ until seven.

8. We **saw** a great movie about frogs. Have you _____ it yet?

9. I'll **tell** you the silly joke that my cousin _____ me.

10. Can you **write** another poem as fine as the one you

_____ about the sunset?

For each sentence, write an ending that tells what is happening in the picture.

The **predicate** of a sentence tells what happens.

1. The cat _____ .

2. The mouse _____ .

3. The cat _____ .

4. The mouse _____ .

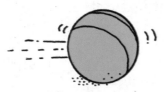

5. The ball _____ .

6. The milk _____ .

Look at the noun *arrow* at the top of the triangle at right. Then read each line. The adjectives are underlined. Note how they help to tell more about the arrow.

> An **adjective** is a word that describes a noun. An adjective often tells what kind or how many.

arrow

<u>red</u> arrow

<u>sleek</u> <u>red</u> arrow

<u>straight</u> <u>sleek</u> <u>red</u> arrow

Complete the triangles below.
Add adjectives on each line to describe the nouns.

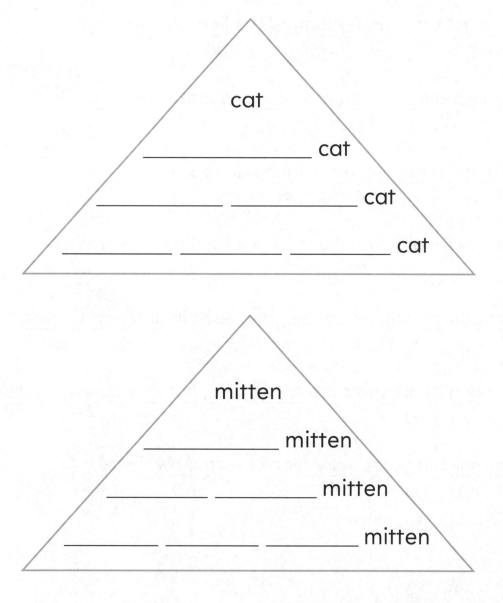

cat

_____ cat

_____ _____ cat

_____ _____ _____ cat

mitten

_____ mitten

_____ _____ mitten

_____ _____ _____ mitten

Mark the letter of the word that is an adjective.

1. Our <u>sun</u> <u>is</u> really a <u>special</u> <u>star</u>.
   Ⓐ Ⓑ   Ⓒ   Ⓓ

2. <u>It</u> is a huge, <u>fiery</u> <u>ball</u> <u>in</u> the universe.
   Ⓐ   Ⓑ   Ⓒ Ⓓ

3. The <u>sun</u> is <u>so</u> <u>hot</u> that it <u>can</u> heat the earth.
   Ⓐ   Ⓑ Ⓒ   Ⓓ

4. The <u>bright</u> sun is hotter <u>than</u> all the <u>fires</u> on <u>earth</u>.
   Ⓐ   Ⓑ   Ⓒ   Ⓓ

5. <u>Too</u> much sun can <u>burn</u> your <u>skin</u> and make you <u>sick</u>.
   Ⓐ   Ⓑ   Ⓒ   Ⓓ

6. The <u>moon</u> is <u>our</u> <u>nearest</u> <u>neighbor</u> in space.
   Ⓐ   Ⓑ   Ⓒ   Ⓓ

7. <u>Brave</u> <u>men</u> walked <u>on</u> the moon for the first <u>time</u> in 1969.
   Ⓐ   Ⓑ   Ⓒ   Ⓓ

8. <u>During</u> the <u>month</u>, we can see the moon in <u>different</u> <u>shapes</u>.
   Ⓐ   Ⓑ   Ⓒ   Ⓓ

9. The moon's <u>dark</u> spots are <u>called</u> seas, <u>but</u> <u>they</u> have no water.
   Ⓐ   Ⓑ   Ⓒ Ⓓ

10. Moon <u>soil</u> is <u>much</u> too <u>dry</u> for plants to <u>grow</u> there.
    Ⓐ   Ⓑ   Ⓒ   Ⓓ

Adjectives are words that describe. Strong adjectives spark the imagination. They give readers clear pictures in their minds as they read. Use active adjectives to make your writing more interesting.

Okay: *She sat under a tree.*
Better: *She sat under a leafy tree.*

Think about each word in the web. In the spaces around it, write adjectives to describe the word.

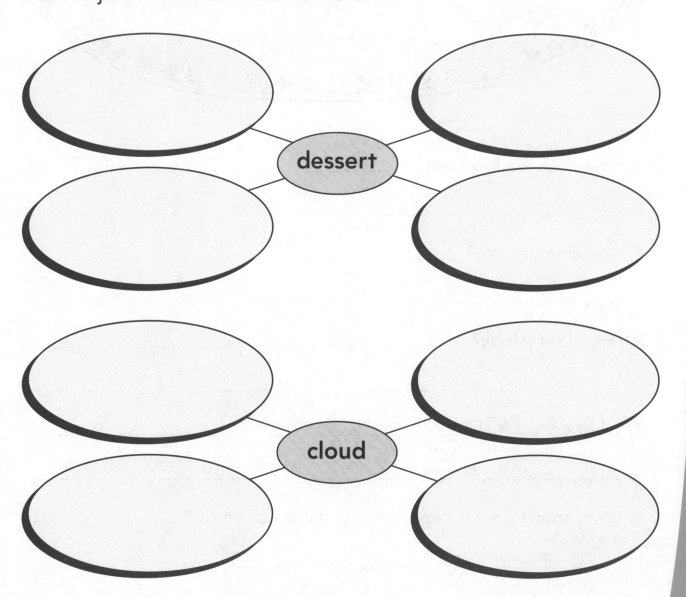

dessert

cloud

Choose one of the types of food listed below. Circle its name on the dish. Then write adjectives to describe how the food smells, tastes, looks, feels, and sounds.

popcorn	peach	pumpkin pie
pineapple	potato	peas
peanut butter	pizza	peppermint candy
pudding	pear	pretzel

1. How does the food smell? _____

_____

2. How does it taste? _____

_____

3. How does it look? _____

_____

4. What does it feel like? _____

_____

5. What sound does it make when you cook or eat it? _____

_____

Fill in the chart. Add **-er** and **-est** to each base word. Think about spelling changes you may need to make. The first row is done for you.

RULES
- Drop silent e
- Change y to i

Base Word	-er	-est
fast	fast**er**	fast**est**
high		
small		
safe		
silly		
new		
cold		
early		
dark		
brave		

The word in **boldface** is an adjective. Write a different form of the adjective to complete each sentence. The first one has been done for you.

1. Diego can run **fast**, but Carl is even _____faster_____.

2. Shelly is **older** than Rose, but Patty is the _____.

3. A cow is a **big** animal, but a moose is _____.

4. Her eyes are _____ than the **bluest** ocean.

5. I got a **short** hair cut, but my brother got an even _____ cut.

6. The **funny** joke became _____ when he told it with a squeaky voice.

7. If one balloon makes you **happy**, will two balloons make you _____ ?

8. Mom was **busy** before, but with the new baby she is _____ than ever.

9. The wind is blowing **hard** today, but it blew _____ last night.

10. Sarah is **taller** than me, but Marci is the _____ kid in our class.

Adverbs can tell *how, when, where, how often,* or *how much.* Many adverbs end in *-ly.*

Okay: *It rains in the desert.*

Better: *It <u>rarely</u> rains in the desert.* [how often]
           It rains <u>monthly</u> in the desert. [when]

> An **adverb** is a word that describes a verb or an adjective.

Read the sentences below.
Write if the adverb tells *how, when, where, how often,* or *how much.*

1. It gets **very** hot in the desert.

_____

2. Desert animals **usually** hide in the shade during the day.

_____

3. Many desert animals come **out** at night.

_____

4. Sometimes it rains **heavily** in deserts.

_____

5. The water **quickly** disappears.

_____

6. We are going to the desert **tomorrow**.

_____

7. I have **never** been to the desert before.

_____

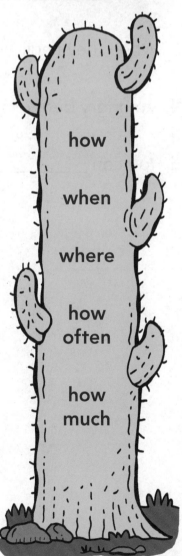

how

when

where

how
often

how
much

Adverbs can tell when, where, how, or how much.
Fill in each blank with an adverb from the box below.

always	hungrily	loudly
quickly	sometimes	usually

1. Bears _____ take a

long sleep in the winter.

2. Bears _____ sleep inside caves.

3. When they finally wake up, bears eat _____.

4. An angry bear growls _____.

5. You can _____ see a real bear in a zoo.

Draw lines to match the *contraction* with two words that mean the same. The first one is done for you.

Contract means "to get smaller."

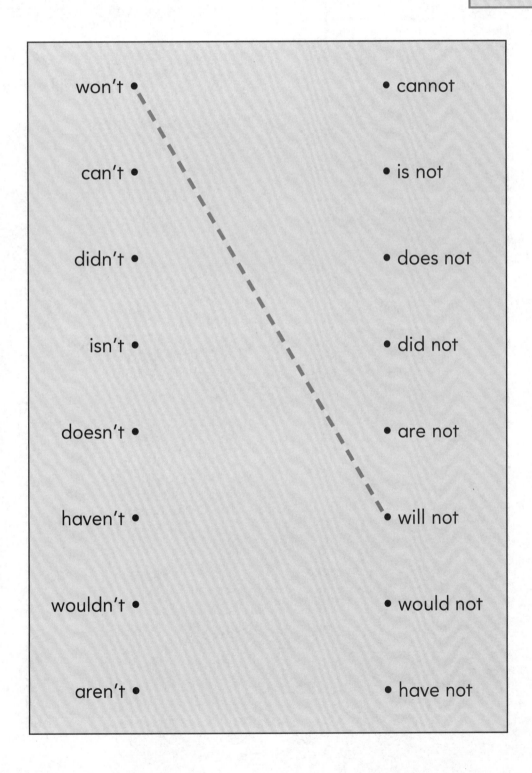

won't • | • cannot
can't • | • is not
didn't • | • does not
isn't • | • did not
doesn't • | • are not
haven't • | • will not
wouldn't • | • would not
aren't • | • have not

Draw lines to match the *contraction* with two words that mean the same. The first one is done for you.

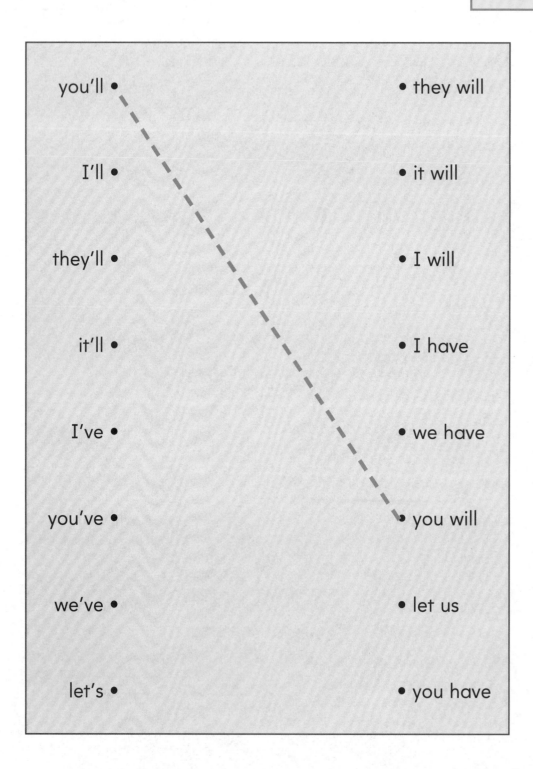

you'll •   • they will

I'll •   • it will

they'll •   • I will

it'll •   • I have

I've •   • we have

you've •   • you will

we've •   • let us

let's •   • you have

In each row, circle the word that is spelled wrong.
If all the words are spelled right, circle *No Mistake.*

1.	middle	midle	riddle	*No Mistake*
2.	large	garage	barje	*No Mistake*
3.	dancing	fencing	forced	*No Mistake*
4.	vacation	action	fraktion	*No Mistake*
5.	sleeve	believe	receive	*No Mistake*
6.	explane	unchain	against	*No Mistake*
7.	breakfast	lunch	dinnor	*No Mistake*
8.	square	skirt	scarf	*No Mistake*
9.	trinket	blankit	thankful	*No Mistake*
10.	measure	pleasant	lether	*No Mistake*
11.	childrun	different	problem	*No Mistake*
12.	meself	ourselves	selfish	*No Mistake*
13.	sugar	ashes	finish	*No Mistake*
14.	gentle	jungle	gardin	*No Mistake*
15.	turkey	monky	skunk	*No Mistake*

Write the missing letters. Use a capital letter where it is needed. Use a lowercase letter where it is needed.

1. H or **h**

_____e plays baseball, but _____is brother plays soccer.

2. D or **d**

We _____id many fun things when we were in _____enver.

3. R or **r**

I live on Maple _____oad, _____ight near the library.

4. L or **l**

The _____ight was so low, _____inda couldn't read her book.

5. W or **w**

I _____onder where _____endy will have her party.

6. T or **t**

I _____ake vitamins every day, but on _____uesday I forgot.

7. I or **i**

My favorite food _____s pizza, but _____ also love shrimp.

8. S or **s**

The knight, _____ir John, was a _____trong warrior.

Write the best end mark. Use **.** or **?** or **!** .

1. Who is your teacher ___

2. Oh, no, my team lost ___

3. Let's meet after school ___

4. Can we get a dog ___

5. Stop right now ___

6. Why is the water running ___

7. It is cool today ___

8. Hey, leave my toys alone ___

9. What is Mom's favorite color ___

10. That was a big problem ___

Read each sentence. Then write another declarative sentence about the picture.

A **declarative** (telling) sentence makes a statement. It begins with a capital letter and ends with a period.

Kim plays in the snow.

1. _____ .

Mark helps Kim.

2. _____ .

The snowman is big.

3. _____ .

The birds sit on the snowman.

4. _____ .

Kim and Mark make a friend for the snowman.

5. _____ .

Look at each picture. Put the words in order to make an interrogative sentence about the picture.

An **interrogative sentence** asks a question. It starts with a capital letter and ends with a question mark.

A Present for Ben

1. put   here   who   basket   this

   _____

2. what   basket   is   inside   the

   _____

3. Ben   hear   what   does

   _____

4. see   does   Ben   what

   _____

5. gave   a   puppy   who   Ben

   _____

Something has just happened in this picture. What is everyone saying? Write a declarative sentence or an interrogative sentence for each speech balloon.

1. _____

2. _____

3. _____

4. _____

5. _____

6. _____

It's often said, "A picture is worth a thousand words." One way to get ideas for writing is to draw a picture. Many writing ideas can come from your own artwork.

Pick a topic. Draw a picture about it. Then list words and ideas on the topic based on your art.

Topic: _____

Words and Ideas:

_____

_____

_____

_____

_____

What is a parka?

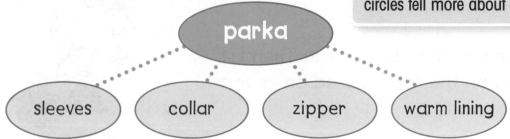

> The **main idea** is the most important idea in a paragraph. In this web, *parka* is the main idea. The words in the smaller circles tell more about the main idea.

Main Idea Sentence: A parka is a warm jacket.

Write a main idea in each web below.
Then, write a main idea sentence.

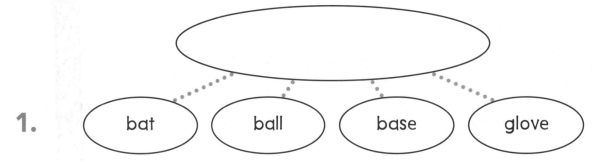

1.

Main Idea Sentence _____

_____

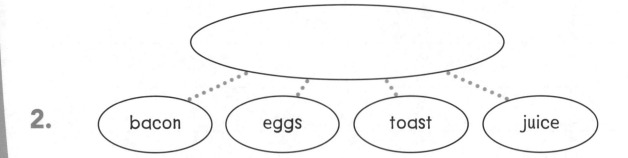

2.

Main Idea Sentence _____

_____

1. Write a main idea in the web below.
Then, write a main idea sentence.

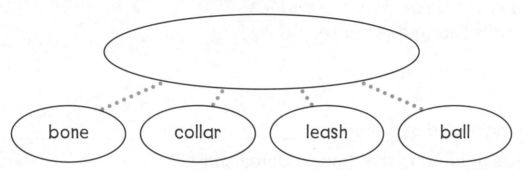

Main Idea Sentence _____

_____

2. Fill in the web with a main idea and information about it.
Then, write a main idea sentence. Choose from the topics
in the Idea Box or think of one of your own.

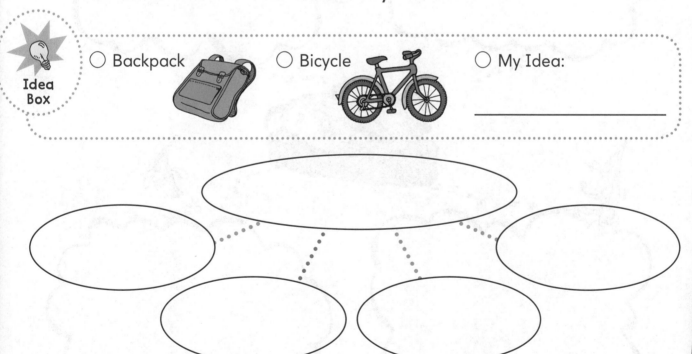

Main Idea Sentence _____

_____

Everybody dreams. But the details
from a dream can be unclear.
Use the chart below to collect ideas.
Add details that make sense.

> **Supporting details** tell
> more about a main idea.

Tell the main idea of a dream: _____

List words or ideas in the dreamy detail chart.

The pictures below tell a story in order.

A story makes sense when you tell the events in the order, or **sequence,** that they happened.

1

2

3

4

A. Number the sentences 1 to 4 to show the best order.

_____ Mr. Silva went to the store.   _____ Mr. Silva filled his cart.

_____ Mr. Silva paid at the counter.   _____ Mr. Silva made a list.

B. Number the pictures 1 to 4 to show the best order.
   Then, write a sentence for each picture, starting with number 1.

_____

_____

_____

_____

A. Number each set of sentences 1 to 4 to show the best order.

1.

_____ Troy got a sponge.

_____ Troy poured some more milk.

_____ Troy cleaned up the milk.

_____ Troy spilled his milk.

2.

_____ Dad bought some popcorn.

_____ Dad and Jen found seats.

_____ Dad and Jen watched the movie.

_____ Dad paid for the tickets.

B. Number the pictures 1 to 4 to show the best order.
Then, write a sentence for each picture, starting with number 1.

_____

_____

_____

_____

Use the pictures to tell a story.

- Focus on your writing purpose.
- Write a good opening sentence.
- Write four sentences in order to tell what is happening.

Writing Purpose _____

_____

Opening Sentence _____

_____

Sentences in Order _____

_____

_____

_____

_____

_____

When you **exaggerate**, you s-t-r-e-t-c-h the truth. Exaggeration makes things seem much bigger or smaller. It can make things seem much better or worse. Exaggeration can be funny or exciting.

Plain: *Kenny was very hungry.*

Exaggerated: *Kenny wanted to eat 50 hot dogs and a watermelon.*

Make each sentence better by exaggerating. It's fine to be funny! The first one has been done for you.

1. The hat was too big on me. <u>The hat was so big, my whole family</u>

<u>could snuggle under it at the same time.</u>

2. Hamid told a funny joke. _____

_____

3. Sally had a sore throat. _____

_____

4. We waited so long! _____

_____

5. That was a dull game. _____

_____

Read each plain sentence. Think about how to make it more lively and more fun to read. Then rewrite the sentence.

1. There were clouds in the sky.

_____

_____

2. The horse walked along the trail.

_____

_____

3. They watched the parade.

_____

_____

4. The doorbell rang.

_____

_____

5. Where did we leave that map?

_____

_____

Choose the sentence in each group that sounds the best.

1. Ⓐ The sun looks like an orange ball.
   Ⓑ Like an orange ball looks the sun.
   Ⓒ An orange ball the sun looks like.

2. Ⓐ Outside my window a nest built by birds.
   Ⓑ Birds outside my window built a nest.
   Ⓒ Birds built a nest outside my window.

3. Ⓐ Dan goes to bed earlier always than do I.
   Ⓑ Dan always goes to bed earlier than I do.
   Ⓒ Dan goes always to bed earlier I do than.

4. Ⓐ Do you like that new book?
   Ⓑ That new book, do you like?
   Ⓒ Do you that new book like?

5. Ⓐ The ranger of the cave took us on a tour.
   Ⓑ Of the cave the ranger on a tour took us.
   Ⓒ The ranger took us on a tour of the cave.

6. Ⓐ I like of my cat to draw pictures.
   Ⓑ I like to draw pictures of my cat.
   Ⓒ My cat to draw pictures I like.

7. Ⓐ Pancakes that looked like stars made Dad.
   Ⓑ Dad made stars that looked like pancakes.
   Ⓒ Dad made pancakes that looked like stars.

8. Ⓐ Sometimes we have eggs for supper.
   Ⓑ We have sometimes eggs for supper.
   Ⓒ Sometimes for supper have we eggs.

Vocabulary

A **synonym** is a word that means the same or almost the same as another word.

Word Bank

argue	choose
exit	glide
keep	rush
shut	slice
trace	wish

Read each sentence.
Trace the word.
Then read the sentences again.

1. To **argue** means to fight using words. _argue_

2. When you **choose** something, you pick the one you want. _choose_

3. To **exit** a place means to leave it. _exit_

4. To **glide** means to move smoothly and easily. _glide_

5. When you **keep** something, you save it. _keep_

6. You **rush** when you are in a hurry. _rush_

7. When you **shut** a door, you close it. _shut_

8. When you **slice** bread, you cut it into thin pieces. _slice_

9. To **trace** something, you follow the lines to copy it. _trace_

10. When you **wish** for something, you hope it will happen. _wish_

A. Write the word that means the same as the word in parentheses.

Word Bank

argue	choose
exit	glide
keep	rush
shut	slice
trace	wish

1. I saw the bird (fly) _____ in the sky.

2. I (want) _____ to go to the moon.

3. My mother likes to (save) _____ the pictures I draw.

4. We always (close) _____ the window when it rains.

5. When my sisters can't agree, sometimes they (fight) _____.

6. When the movie was over, we had to (leave) _____ the theater.

B. Cross out the word in each row that does not belong.

1.	cut	slice	slip
2.	creep	rush	speed
3.	choose	pick	wind
4.	face	draw	trace

A **synonym** is a word that means the same or almost the same as another word.

Read each sentence.
Trace the word.
Then read the sentences again.

Word Bank

breezy	bright
cozy	damp
grumpy	hefty
icy	puzzled
sleepy	simple

1. The wind blows on a **breezy** day. breezy

2. A **bright** day is one that has a lot of light. bright

3. When you are **cozy**, you feel snug and warm. cozy

4. When something is **damp**, it is a bit wet. damp

5. When you feel **grumpy**, you are
   unhappy and in a bad mood. grumpy

6. Something **hefty** is large or strong. hefty

7. An **icy** day is one that is very, very cold. icy

8. When you feel **puzzled**, you are
   confused, or do not understand something. puzzled

9. When you feel **sleepy**, you are tired. sleepy

10. When something is **simple**, it is easy. simple

Read the clues. Write the word next to its clue. Find and circle the word in the puzzle.

Word Bank

breezy	bright	cozy	damp	grumpy
hefty	icy	puzzled	sleepy	simple

1. big and heavy

_____

2. snug and warm

_____

3. tired _____

4. confused _____

5. a little wet _____

6. with a lot of sunlight

_____

7. unhappy _____

8. easy _____

9. a bit windy

_____

10. freezing cold _____

B	R	I	G	H	T	B	V	L	E
R	X	N	R	E	P	K	I	O	H
E	T	I	G	R	U	M	P	Y	E
E	W	S	I	L	Z	U	B	T	F
Z	A	D	C	O	Z	Y	A	I	T
Y	I	A	Y	S	L	E	E	P	Y
S	I	M	P	L	E	X	X	T	G
Q	U	P	S	S	D	S	S	Y	S

An **antonym** is a word that means the opposite of another word.

Read each sentence.
Trace the word.
Then read the sentences again.

Word Bank

fix ⟷ wreck

frown ⟷ smile

hide ⟷ show

whisper ⟷ yell

weep ⟷ laugh

1. When you **fix** something, you put it back together. fix

2. When you **wreck** something, you break it. wreck

3. When you feel sad, you **frown**. frown

4. When you feel happy, you **smile**. smile

5. When you **hide** something, people cannot see it. hide

6. When you **show** something, people can see it. show

7. When you **whisper**, you speak quietly. whisper

8. When you **yell**, you speak loudly. yell

9. When you think something is very sad, you **weep**. weep

10. When you think something is funny, you **laugh**. laugh

A. Write the best word to complete
   each sentence.

> ## Word Bank
>
> fix ⟷ wreck
> frown ⟷ smile
> hide ⟷ show
> whisper ⟷ yell
> weep ⟷ laugh

1. When my mom hugs me, I _____.

2. We _____ loudly when our
   team makes a good play.

3. I _____ when I am sad and grumpy.

4. When the teacher tells a joke, the children _____.

5. I _____ when I don't want to wake up my brother.

6. Our parents _____ the presents so we can't find them.

7. The deer _____ the garden when they eat the flowers.

B. Write the word that is the antonym of each picture.

1. _____

2. _____

3. _____

An **antonym** is a word that means the opposite of another word.

Read each sentence.
Trace the word.
Then read the sentences again.

Word Bank

bland ⟷ spicy

dark ⟷ light

early ⟷ late

huge ⟷ tiny

loud ⟷ quiet

1. Food that tastes plain is **bland**. bland

2. **Spicy** food has a lot of flavor. spicy

3. At night, it is **dark** outside. dark

4. In the day, it is **light** outside. light

5. When you are **early**, you arrive before something starts. early

6. When you are **late**, you arrive after something starts. late

7. Something very, very big is **huge**. huge

8. Something very, very small is **tiny**. tiny

9. When there is a lot of noise, it is **loud**. loud

10. When there is no noise, it is **quiet**. quiet

Read the word on each puzzle piece.
Draw a line to match each word with
an antonym.

1.  light

 spicy

2. 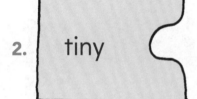 tiny

 quiet

3. 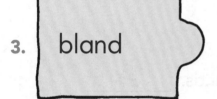 bland

 dark

4. 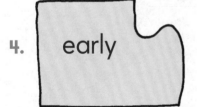 early

 late

5. 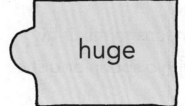 loud

huge

A **verb** describes an action.

Think about how the verbs are alike and how they are different.

Read each sentence.
Trace the word.
Then read the sentences again.

1. To **creep** is to walk very slowly. creep

2. To **stroll** is to walk at a medium pace. stroll

3. To **rest** is to stay quiet and relax. rest

4. To **nap** is to sleep for a short time. nap

5. To **take** means to get something using your hands. take

6. To **grab** means to take something quickly. grab

7. To **turn** means to move in a circle. turn

8. To **spin** means to turn quickly, many times. spin

9. To **stir** something means to mix it by moving it around with a spoon or a stick. stir

10. To **whisk** something means to stir it quickly in one direction. whisk

A. Write the best word to complete
each sentence.

creep	stroll
rest	nap
take	grab
turn	spin
stir	whisk

1. I always _____ my lunch
to school.

2. I need to _____ after I
run a lot.

3. I saw a spider _____ up the wall.

4. Watch the baby, or he may _____ the dog's tail.

5. We like to _____ in circles and fall down
on the grass.

6. The water will come out of the faucet when you _____
the handle.

B. Read each question. Check ✔ the best answer.

1. Which food would you **stir**? ☐ crackers ☐ soup

2. Which food would you **whisk**? ☐ eggs ☐ toast

3. Where would you **stroll**? ☐ park ☐ pool

4. Where would you **nap**? ☐ kitchen ☐ bedroom

A **verb** describes an action.

Think about how the verbs are alike and how they are different.

Word Bank

climb	nibble
peek	pounce
scurry	stare
stretch	surprise
wiggle	worry

Read each sentence.
Trace the word.
Then read the sentences again.

1. When you **climb**, you go to a higher place. climb

2. To **nibble** is to take very small bites. nibble

3. To **peek** is to look at something quickly. peek

4. To **pounce** is to jump on something quickly. pounce

5. To **scurry** is to run with short, quick steps. scurry

6. When you **stare**, you look at something for a long time. stare

7. To **stretch** is to spread out a part of your body. stretch

8. To **surprise** is to do something without warning. surprise

9. When you **wiggle**, you make small movements from side to side or up and down. wiggle

10. When you **worry**, you think something bad might happen. worry

Read the clues. Write the word next to its clue. Find and circle the word in the puzzle.

Word Bank

| climb | nibble | peek | pounce | scurry |
| stare | stretch | surprise | wiggle | worry |

1. look for a long time _____

2. eat small bites _____

3. move around _____

4. shock or startle _____

5. run away _____

6. feel upset _____

7. jump on _____

8. a quick look _____

9. go up high _____

10. spread out _____

```
W I G G L E S U R P
O P S T R E T C H O
R E W B B L A L S U
R E I M T Y R I C N
Y K M P S G E M U C
N I B B L E L B R E
S U R P R I S E R C
O P T C H Q U D Y G
```

A **verb** describes an action.

Think about how the verbs are alike and how they are different.

Word Bank

crawl	fade
fasten	flutter
gaze	scoot
soar	sprinkle
twist	yank

Read each sentence.
Trace the word.
Then read the sentences again.

1. To **crawl** means to move on your hands and knees. crawl

2. To **fade** means to lose color. fade

3. To **fasten** means to attach one thing to something else. fasten

4. To **flutter** means to wave or flap something. flutter

5. To **gaze** at something means
   to look at it for a period of time. gaze

6. To **scoot** is a way to move quickly. scoot

7. To **soar** is to fly very high in the air. soar

8. To **sprinkle** is to scatter something in small drops or bits. sprinkle

9. To **twist** means to turn or bend something. twist

10. To **yank** means to pull something in a sharp way. yank

Read the clues. Write the vocabulary word.
Use the answers in the boxes to complete
the puzzle below.

Word Bank

crawl	fade
fasten	flutter
gaze	scoot
soar	sprinkle
twist	yank

1. to look at for a long time _ ☐ _ _

2. how babies move around ☐ _ _ _ _

3. to hook or button _ _ _ ☐ _ _

4. to pour a little bit _ _ _ ☐ _ _ _ _

5. to move quickly _ _ ☐ _ _

6. to pull sharply _ _ ☐ _

7. to turn something around _ ☐ _ _ _

8. how birds move high in the sky _ ☐ _ _

9. how a flag might move in the wind _ _ _ _ _ _ ☐

10. to lose color _ _ ☐ _

What is a verb?

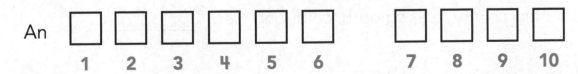

An ☐ ☐ ☐ ☐ ☐ ☐   ☐ ☐ ☐ ☐
    1   2   3   4   5   6   7   8   9 10

These words all describe a **texture**, or how something feels (or looks).

Word Bank

chewy	crumbly
creamy	foamy
furry	gritty
rough	sharp
slimy	wrinkled

Think about how the words are alike and how they are different.

Read each sentence.
Trace the word.
Then read the sentences again.

1. Something **chewy** can get stuck in your teeth.   chewy

2. When something is **crumbly**, it falls apart easily.   crumbly

3. When something is **creamy**, it is very soft and smooth.   creamy

4. Something **foamy** has a lot of small bubbles in it.   foamy

5. When something is **furry**, it has soft, thick hair.   furry

6. When something is **gritty**, it feels like sand.   gritty

7. When something is **rough**, there are bumps on its surface.   rough

8. When something is **sharp**, it has a pointed end.   sharp

9. Something **slimy** feels smooth, cold, and wet.   slimy

10. When something is **wrinkled**,
    it has a lot of folds or lines.   wrinkled

A. Write the best word to complete
   each sentence.

Word Bank

chewy	crumbly
creamy	foamy
furry	gritty
rough	sharp
slimy	wrinkled

1. I like to pet the _____ kitten.

2. Bubbles in the bathtub are _____.

3. Dad ironed the _____ clothes.

4. When I touched the frog, it felt _____.

5. Peanut butter can be _____ or crunchy.

6. Mom told us to be careful with the _____ scissors.

B. Read each question. Check ✔ the best answer.

1. What feels **gritty**? ☐ beach ☐ swings

2. What feels **rough**? ☐ tree bark ☐ window

3. Which one is **crumbly**? ☐ cookie ☐ lollipop

4. Which one is **chewy**? ☐ ice cream ☐ gum

These words all describe **sounds**.

Word Bank

achoo	chirp
click	crackle
ding	plink
quack	splash
squeak	whoosh

Think about how the sound words are alike and how they are different.

Read each sentence.
Trace the word.
Then read the sentences again.

1. **Achoo** is the sound you make when you sneeze. <u>achoo</u>

2. A **chirp** is the sound you hear when a bird sings. <u>chirp</u>

3. A **click** is a sharp, quick sound. <u>click</u>

4. Dry leaves **crackle** when you walk on them. <u>crackle</u>

5. When a timer goes off, you hear a **ding**. <u>ding</u>

6. A **plink** is the sound rain makes when it hits the roof. <u>plink</u>

7. A **quack** is the sound a duck makes. <u>quack</u>

8. When a frog jumps into water, you hear a **splash**. <u>splash</u>

9. A **squeak** is a very short, high noise. <u>squeak</u>

10. When something goes by you very fast, you hear a **whoosh**. <u>whoosh</u>

Look at the pictures. Write the best
sound word for each one.

Word Bank

achoo	chirp
click	crackle
ding	plink
quack	splash
squeak	whoosh

1. _____

2. _____

3. _____

4. _____

5. _____

6. _____

7. _____

8. _____

9. _____

10. _____

A **homophone** is a word that sounds like another word but has a different meaning and a different spelling.

Read each sentence.
Trace the word.
Then read the sentences again.

1. A **hole** is a place where there is an empty space. hole

2. **Whole** means all of something, with nothing missing. whole

3. When two things match, they are a **pair**. pair

4. A **pear** is a sweet fruit that is bigger
   around the bottom than at the top. pear

5. To **rap** on something means to knock on it. rap

6. When you **wrap** a gift, you cover it in pretty paper. wrap

7. To **sail** means to move on water using the power of the wind. sail

8. A **sale** is a time when a store sells
   things for less than they usually cost. sale

9. To **steal** is to take something that does not belong to you. steal

10. **Steel** is a hard, strong metal that is used to make buildings. steel

A. Write the best word to complete
each sentence.

Word Bank

hole ⟷ whole

pair ⟷ pear

rap ⟷ wrap

sail ⟷ sale

steal ⟷ steel

1. The boats _____ in the lake.

2. The ball rolled into a deep _____
and got stuck.

3 The store was having a big _____.

4. Use paper, tape, and ribbon to _____ a present.

5. My two older brothers ate a _____ pizza.

6. We ate a fruit salad, made with
an apple, a banana, and a _____.

B. Read each question. Check ✔ the best answer.

1. Which one describes a **pair**? ☐ sweet ☐ two

2. What do you do when you **rap**? ☐ knock ☐ cover

3. What do people who **steal** do? ☐ take ☐ give

4. Which one is made of **steel**? ☐ cabin ☐ skyscraper

A **homonym** is a word that sounds like another word, and can be spelled the same way, but has a different meaning.

Read each sentence.
Trace the word.
Then read the sentences again.

1. A **ball** is a round object used to play different games. ball

2. A **ball** is a big party where people dance. ball

3. A **bat** is a long hard stick you use to hit a ball. bat

4. A flying animal that feeds at night is called a **bat**. bat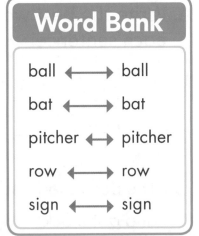

5. In baseball, the **pitcher** throws the ball to the batter. pitcher

6. A **pitcher** is a container that holds something you drink. pitcher

7. A **row** is a line of things or people side by side. row

8. To **row** a boat, you use oars to make it move through water. row

9. A **sign** is writing or a picture that gives you information. sign

10. When you write your name on something, you **sign** it. sign

A. Write the best word to complete
   each sentence.

Word Bank

ball ⟷ ball

bat ⟷ bat

pitcher ⟷ pitcher

row ⟷ row

sign ⟷ sign

1. I put my stuffed animals

   in a _____ on the shelf.

2. The baseball player held a _____

   made of wood.

3. Cinderella dressed up and went to a _____ .

4. The _____ threw the _____ to the batter.

5. I remembered to _____ my name at the bottom

   of the letter.

6. Let's _____ the boat to the other side of the lake.

B. Read each question. Check ✔ the best answer.

1. Can a bat hold a **bat**?   ☐ yes   ☐ no

2. Can a pitcher use a **pitcher**?   ☐ yes   ☐ no

3. Can you sign a **sign**?   ☐ yes   ☐ no

A **compound word** is made up of two smaller words put together.

Read each sentence.
Trace the word.
Then read the sentences again.

Word Bank

birdhouse	cowboy
drumstick	firefly
scarecrow	starfish
sunflower	toothbrush
wheelchair	wristwatch

1. A house for birds is called a **birdhouse**. birdhouse

2. A **cowboy** is someone who looks after cattle. cowboy

3. A **drumstick** is a stick used to play a drum. drumstick

4. A **firefly** is a small flying beetle that lights up at night. firefly

5. A farmer puts a **scarecrow** in a field to keep birds away. scarecrow

6. A **starfish** is a sea animal that looks like a star. starfish

7. A **sunflower** is a large flower with yellow petals and a dark center. sunflower

8. You use a **toothbrush** to clean your teeth. toothbrush

9. A **wheelchair** is a chair that moves on wheels. wheelchair

10. A **wristwatch** fits around your wrist and is used to tell time. wristwatch

Draw a line to match each compound word with its picture.

1.  wristwatch

2.  firefly

3.  birdhouse

4.  scarecrow

5.  sunflower

6.  starfish

7.  wheelchair

8.  cowboy

9.  toothbrush

10.  drumstick

198

A **compound word** is made up of two smaller words put together.

Read each sentence.
Trace the word.
Then read the sentences again.

Word Bank

clothespin	goldfish
grasshopper	greenhouse
headphones	houseboat
playground	sidewalk
snowflake	wallpaper

1. A **clothespin** holds clothes on a line to dry. clothespin

2. A small fish that is gold in color is a **goldfish**. goldfish

3. A **grasshopper** is an insect that hops. grasshopper

4. A **greenhouse** is a glass building in which plants can grow safely. greenhouse

5. You wear **headphones** over your ears to listen to music. headphones

6. A **houseboat** is a kind of boat that people can live in. houseboat

7. A **playground** is a place for children to play outside. playground

8. A **sidewalk** is a path for walking beside a street. sidewalk

9. A small bit of snow is called a **snowflake**. snowflake

10. **Wallpaper** is paper used to decorate a wall. wallpaper

Think of a word for each picture.
Then write the compound word.

Word Bank

clothespin	goldfish
grasshopper	greenhouse
headphones	houseboat
playground	sidewalk
snowflake	wallpaper

1. [image] + flake = _____

2. gold + [image] = _____

3. [image] + phones = _____

4. wall + [image] = _____

5. [image] + [image] = _____

6. green + [image] = _____

7. [image] + ground = _____

8. side + [image] = _____

9. [image] + hopper = _____

10. [image] + [image] = _____

A **prefix** is a word part that is added to the beginning of a word. A prefix changes the meaning of a word.

The prefix *un-* means "not."
The prefix *re-* means "again."

Read each sentence.
Trace the word.
Then read the sentences again.

Word Bank

uneven	unhappy
unpack	unsafe
untrue	remake
replace	reread
reuse	rewrite

1. Something **uneven** is not level. uneven

2. **Unhappy** means to be sad. unhappy

3. **Unpack** means to empty something, like a suitcase after a trip. unpack

4. Something **unsafe** is dangerous. unsafe

5. Something false is **untrue**. untrue

6. When you **remake** your bed, you make it again. remake

7. When something is missing, you **replace** it. replace

8. When you read a book again, you **reread** it. reread

9. When you use something more than once, you **reuse** it. reuse

10. When you erase a word and write it again, you **rewrite** it. rewrite

A. Write the best word to complete
   each sentence.

Word Bank

uneven	unhappy
unpack	unsafe
untrue	remake
replace	reread
reuse	rewrite

1. I save something so I

   can _____ it.

2. He likes to _____ his favorite books.

3. If you tell a lie, what you say is _____.

4. My sandwich fell apart so I had to _____ it.

5. When my little sister was crying, I knew she was _____.

6. My mom told me that it is _____ to swim in a pool alone.

B. Read each question. Check ✔ the best answer.

1. Which one can you **rewrite**?　　☐ pencil　　☐ story

2. When do you **unpack**?　　☐ after a trip　　☐ before a trip

3. Which one would you **replace**?　　☐ broken toy　　☐ new toy

4. Which one describes　　☐ straight　　☐ crooked
   something **uneven**?

A **suffix** is a word part that is added to the end of a word. A suffix changes the meaning of a word.

Word Bank

careful	colorful
hopeful	joyful
playful	baker
builder	painter
singer	writer

The suffix -*ful* means "full of."

The suffix -*er* means "a person who acts as."

Read each sentence.
Trace the word.
Then read the sentences again.

1. Being **careful** means paying close attention to what you do. _careful_

2. Something **colorful** is made up of many colors. _colorful_

3. Being **hopeful** means that you wish for something. _hopeful_

4. When you are **joyful**, you feel very happy. _joyful_

5. Being **playful** means you like to play and have fun. _playful_

6. A **baker** is a person who bakes foods. _baker_

7. A **builder** is a person whose job it is to build things. _builder_

8. A **painter** is a person who paints. _painter_

9. A **singer** is a person who sings songs. _singer_

10. A **writer** is a person who writes things, like stories. _writer_

Read the clues. Write the word next to its clue. Find and circle the word in the puzzle.

1. someone who sings

_____

2. feeling joy _____

3. someone who paints

_____

4. acting in a fun way

_____

5. someone who makes a cake

_____

6. acting with care

_____

7. feeling hope _____

8. someone who writes a story

_____

9. having a lot of color

_____

10. someone who builds a house

_____

```
I X G B J M H C A R E F U L H
S L E P F U P O R E G U L R W
A P L A Y F U L K E B A K E R
I A O R F D J O Y F U L L T I
S I N G E R A R C L I U R E T
T N R H O P E F U L L D E R E
E T O R F X Y U F U D C X T R
R E T R I Q U L B D E C X T L
I R G B J M H C T M R F U L H
```

Character traits tell what someone is like or how he or she acts.

Word Bank

brave	curious
fair	friendly
gentle	greedy
honest	mean
polite	sneaky

Read each sentence.
Trace the word.
Then read the sentences again.

1. A **brave** person acts strong and without fear. *brave*

2. A **curious** person likes to learn about things. *curious*

3. A **fair** person treats everyone the same way. *fair*

4. A **friendly** person acts nice and helpful. *friendly*

5. A **gentle** person is kind and careful with others. *gentle*

6. A **greedy** person does not like to share with others. *greedy*

7. An **honest** person tells the truth. *honest*

8. A **mean** person is not kind or friendly. *mean*

9. A **polite** person has good manners. *polite*

10. A **sneaky** person tries to do things in secret. *sneaky*

A. Write the best word to complete
   each sentence.

Word Bank

brave	curious
fair	friendly
gentle	greedy
honest	mean
polite	sneaky

1. He never lies. He is _____.

2. My friend was _____ when
he held his new puppy.

3. Our coach makes sure everyone gets to play in the game.

She is _____.

4. She always says "please" and "thank you." She is _____.

5. I read a lot of books because I am _____ about
many things.

6. The _____ firefighter saved the people who were
caught in a fire.

B. Read each question. Check ✔ the best answer.

1. What does a **greedy** person like to do? ☐ take ☐ give

2. What does a **friendly** person's face show? ☐ frown ☐ smile

3. Which one is **mean**? ☐ bully ☐ friend

4. How might a **sneaky** person walk? ☐ tiptoe ☐ stomp

Special words are used to tell about **mealtime**.

Read each sentence.
Trace the word.
Then read the sentences again.

Word Bank	
meal	breakfast
lunch	dinner
drink	dessert
snack	leftovers
kitchen	cafeteria

1. A **meal** is the food we eat at one time. meal

2. **Breakfast** is a meal eaten in the morning. breakfast

3. **Lunch** is a meal eaten in the middle of the day. lunch

4. **Dinner** is a meal eaten in the evening. dinner

5. You have a **drink** when you are thirsty. drink

6. **Dessert** is something sweet eaten after a meal. dessert

7. A **snack** is something you eat between meals. snack

8. The food not eaten at a meal is called **leftovers**.
   You can eat that food at another time. leftovers

9. A **kitchen** is the room where you make a meal. kitchen

10. At school, the **cafeteria** is a place where
    you can eat a meal. cafeteria

Think of the best word to complete each
sentence. Use the Word Bank.
Complete the puzzle.

> ## Word Bank
>
> | | |
> |---|---|
> | meal | breakfast |
> | lunch | dinner |
> | drink | dessert |
> | snack | leftovers |
> | kitchen | cafeteria |

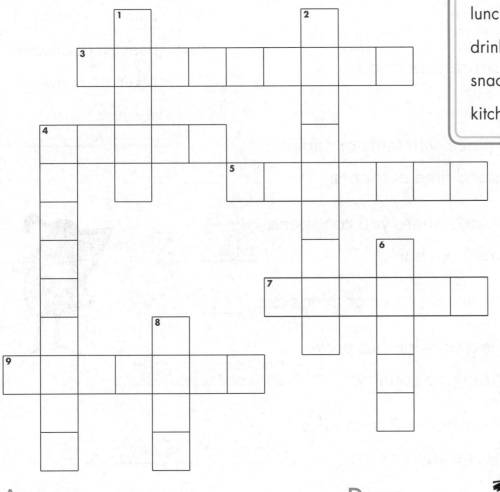

Across

3. I always eat cereal for __.

4. Most days, I take my __ to school.

5. We make food in the __.

7. Sometimes, I can invite a
friend to __.

9. Ice cream makes a good __.

Down

1. Apple juice is my favorite __.

2. At school, I eat in the __.

4. We have some __ in
the refrigerator.

6. I eat a __ before soccer practice.

8. On Thanksgiving, we have
a special __.

Special words are used to tell about a **vacation**.

Word Bank

camp	hotel
map	passport
sleepover	suitcase
ticket	travel
vacation	visit

Read each sentence.
Trace the word.
Then read the sentences again.

1. A **camp** is a place with tents or cabins where you spend time outdoors. camp

2. A **hotel** is a place where you can spend the night away from home. hotel

3. A **map** shows where places or things are. map

4. A **passport** is a booklet that proves you are a citizen of a country. passport

5. A **sleepover** is when you spend the night at someone else's house. sleepover

6. A **suitcase** is a bag to carry clothes in when you travel. suitcase

7. A **ticket** is a piece of paper that shows you have paid to do something. ticket

8. To **travel** is to go from one place to another place. travel

9. **Vacation** is time away from school or work. vacation

10. To **visit** is to go somewhere or see someone. visit

A. Write the best word to complete each sentence.

1. I like to _____ my grandparents.

2. We stayed at a _____ when we went to the city.

3. I like to _____ to different places.

4. During the summer, my family goes on a _____.

5. When we go to a _____, we sleep in our sleeping bags.

6. On the weekend, I sometimes have a _____ at my friend's house.

B. Write the word that goes with each picture.

1.  _____

2.  _____

3.  _____

4.  _____

Special words are used for different kinds of **land** formations and bodies of **water**.

Read each sentence.
Trace the word.
Then read the sentences again.

Word Bank

cave	dune
hill	lake
ocean	pond
mountain	range
river	stream

1. A **cave** is an open space in the side of a mountain or under the ground. cave

2. A **dune** is a mound of sand made by blowing winds. dune

3. A **hill** is a place where the land rises above the area around it. hill

4. A **lake** is water with land all around it. lake

5. An **ocean** is a very large body of saltwater. ocean

6. A **pond** is water with land all around it. It is smaller than a lake. pond

7. A **mountain** is a very high hill. mountain

8. A **range** is a group of mountains. range

9. A **river** is a large body of flowing water. river

10. A **stream** is a small river. stream

Some of the words name land formations.
Others name bodies of water.
Sort the words in the Word Bank into
two groups. Write them in the chart.

Word Bank

cave	dune
hill	lake
ocean	pond
mountain	range
river	stream

Land Words

_____

_____

_____

_____

Water Words

_____

_____

_____

_____

Special words are used to describe different kinds of **weather**.

Word Bank

blizzard	dust storm
flood	fog
hail	heat wave
hurricane	sleet
thunderstorm	tornado

Read each sentence.
Trace the word.
Then read the sentences again.

1. A **blizzard** is a very heavy snowstorm. <u>blizzard</u>

2. A **dust storm** happens when strong winds
   blow dust, soil, or sand around a large area. <u>dust storm</u>

3. When an area overflows with water, it is called a **flood**. <u>flood</u>

4. **Fog** is a low, thick cloud of water droplets. <u>fog</u>

5. **Hail** is made of small balls of ice that fall from the sky. <u>hail</u>

6. A **heat wave** is very hot weather
   that lasts a few days. <u>heat wave</u>

7. A **hurricane** is a strong storm with
   high winds that starts over the ocean. <u>hurricane</u>

8. **Sleet** is rain that is partly frozen. <u>sleet</u>

9. A **thunderstorm** is a storm with
   thunder and lightning. <u>thunderstorm</u>

10. A **tornado** is a powerful storm with strong winds
    that spin in the shape of a cone. <u>tornado</u>

Trace a path through the maze.
Follow the weather words.

Word Bank

blizzard	dust storm
flood	fog
hail	heat wave
hurricane	sleet
thunderstorm	tornado

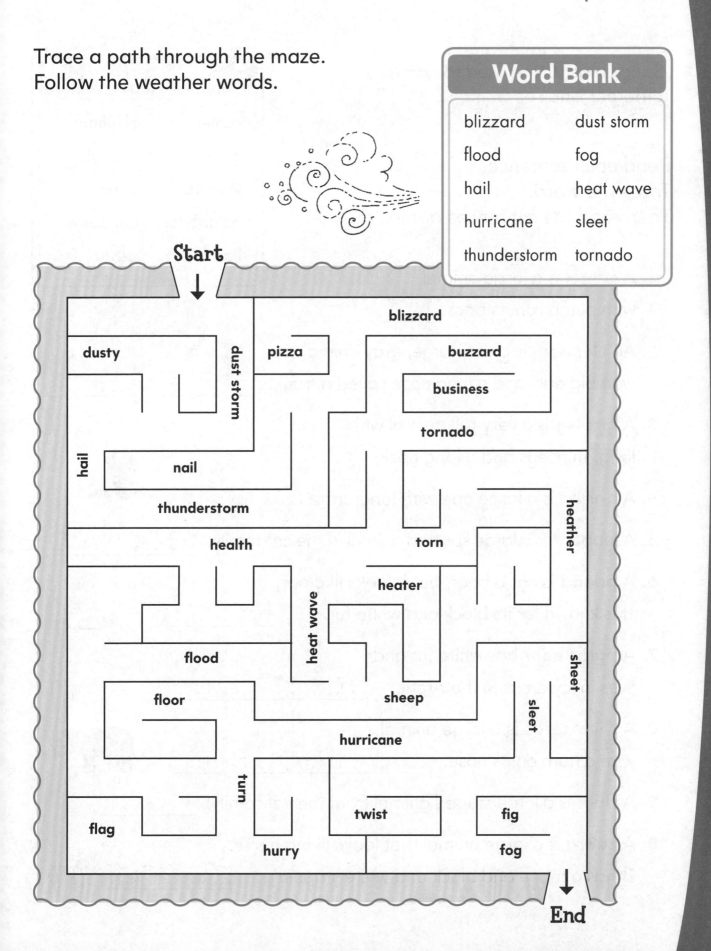

Start

blizzard

dusty
pizza
buzzard

business

dust storm

tornado

hail

nail

heather

thunderstorm

health
torn

heater

heat wave

flood

sheet

floor

sleet

sheep

hurricane

turn

flag
twist
fig

hurry
fog

End

214

Special words are used to name different kinds of **animals**.

Word Bank

camel	elephant
giraffe	gorilla
leopard	panda
polar bear	rhinoceros
tiger	zebra

Read each sentence.
Trace the word.
Then read the sentences again.

1. A **camel** is a large animal
   with humps on its back. camel

2. An **elephant** is a very large, gray animal
   with big ears and a long nose called a trunk. elephant

3. A **giraffe** is a very tall animal with
   long, thin legs and a long neck. giraffe

4. A **gorilla** is a large ape with long arms. gorilla

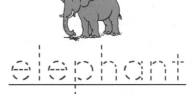

5. A **leopard** is a large spotted animal in the cat family. leopard

6. A **panda** is not a bear, but it looks like one.
   It is known for its black and white fur. panda

7. A **polar bear** has white fur and
   lives in icy areas in the Arctic. polar bear

8. A **rhinoceros** is a large animal
   with a horn on its nose. rhinoceros

9. A **tiger** is a large striped animal from the cat family. tiger

10. A **zebra** is a large animal that looks like a horse.
    It has a mane and black and white stripes. zebra

A. Write the best word to complete each sentence.

Word Bank

camel	elephant
giraffe	gorilla
leopard	panda
polar bear	rhinoceros
tiger	zebra

1. The _____'s fur keeps it warm on the ice.

2. An _____ can hold water in its trunk.

3. A _____ can hold water in its humps.

4. The _____ has stripes and a mane.

5. A _____ is a large, wild cat with stripes.

6. The _____ is black and white and eats bamboo.

B. Read each question. Check ✔ the best answer.

1. Which one is in the cat family? ☐ leopard   ☐ camel

2. Which one has long arms? ☐ gorilla   ☐ giraffe

3. Which one has a horn? ☐ elephant   ☐ rhinoceros

4. Which one is taller? ☐ giraffe   ☐ tiger

Special words are used to name things you might find in a **garden**.

Read each sentence.
Trace the word.
Then read the sentences again.

Word Bank	
bloom	bush
grass	hose
leaves	mower
rake	shovel
soil	worm

1. When flowers **bloom**, they open up. bloom

2. A **bush** is a plant with branches. It is smaller than a tree. bush

3. **Grass** is a green plant that spreads across the ground. grass

4. A **hose** is a long rubber tube that water goes through. hose

5. **Leaves** grow on plants and trees. They are usually green. leaves

6. You use a **mower** to cut grass. mower

7. A **rake** is a tool with a long handle and metal teeth used to gather fallen leaves. rake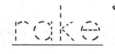

8. A **shovel** is a tool with a handle and a scoop on the end. shovel

9. **Soil** is the top layer of earth that plants grow in. soil

10. A **worm** is a long, thin, soft animal that lives in the ground. worm

Write the word that goes with each picture.
Use the Word Bank.

Word Bank	
bloom	bush
grass	hose
leaves	mower
rake	shovel
soil	worm

1. _____

2. _____

3. _____

4. _____

5. _____

6. _____

7. _____

8. _____

9. _____

10. _____

Special words are used to tell about **money**.

Word Bank

cash	coin
penny	nickel
dime	quarter
half-dollar	dollar bill
price	change

Read each sentence.
Trace the word.
Then read the sentences again.

1. **Cash** is money. It includes coins and dollar bills. cash

2. A **coin** is a piece of metal that is used as money. coin

3. A **penny** is a small metal coin that equals 1 cent. penny

4. A **nickel** is a small metal coin that equals 5 cents. nickel

5. A **dime** is a very small metal coin that equals 10 cents. dime

6. A **quarter** is a metal coin that equals 25 cents. quarter

7. A **half-dollar** is a large metal coin that equals 50 cents. half-dollar

8. A **dollar bill** is paper money. It equals 100 cents. dollar bill

9. The **price** is how much money something costs. price

10. **Change** is money you get back when you pay too much for something. change

A. Write the word that goes with each picture.

1. _____

2. _____

3. _____

4. _____

5. _____

6. _____

B. Read each question. Check ✔ the best answer.

1. Which one tells how much something costs? ☐ change ☐ price

2. Which one could you find in a pocket? ☐ cash ☐ price

3. Which one tells about money you get back? ☐ price ☐ change

4. Which one makes more noise when it hits the floor? ☐ coin ☐ dollar bill

Special words are used for different units and tools of **linear measurement**.

measure	inch
foot	yard
mile	centimeter
meter	ruler
yardstick	meter stick

Read each sentence.
Trace the word.
Then read the sentences again.

1. When you **measure** something, you find out about its size.   measure

2. An **inch** is a small unit of length.   ONE INCH   inch

3. A **foot** is equal to 12 inches.   foot

4. A **yard** is equal to three feet.   yard

5. A **mile** is equal to 5,280 feet. It is used to measure distance.   mile

6. A **centimeter** is a small metric unit.   ONE CENTIMETER   centimeter

7. A **meter** is a metric unit equal to 100 centimeters.   meter

8. To measure 12 inches, you use a **ruler**.   ruler

9. To measure 3 feet, you use a **yardstick**.   yardstick

10. To measure a centimeter or a meter, you use a **meter stick**. A meter stick is a little longer than a yardstick.   meter stick

Sort nine words in the Word Bank
into two groups.
Write them in the chart.

Word Bank

centimeter	yardstick
ruler	meter
mile	inch
meter stick	yard
foot	measure

Units of Measure	Tools Used to Measure

Which word did you not use? _____

Here are some vocabulary words you learned. Use at least seven of these words to write a story below.

Word Bank

glide	slimy
pounce	camp
crackle	cash
brave	spicy
rhinoceros	row
hefty	reuse
sprinkle	dune
wheelchair	mile
dessert	stroll
tornado	pair
hopeful	laugh
houseboat	hose

Math

Write each number.

eight		three	
five		four	
nine		one	
seven		six	
ten		two	

Draw lines to match words to numbers.

eleven	17	fourteen	19
fifteen	20	eighteen	16
twenty	13	sixteen	14
seventeen	15	nineteen	12
thirteen	11	twelve	18

Add. Circle any answer that is your age.

4 + 2 = _____   3 + 2 = _____   1 + 7 = _____

3 + 4 = _____   5 + 1 = _____   2 + 6 = _____

6 + 3 = _____   7 + 2 = _____   5 + 5 = _____

Add. Circle any answer that is 19.

4 + 7 = _____   8 + 8 = _____   9 + 7 = _____

10 + 9 = _____   5 + 7 = _____   7 + 6 = _____

8 + 9 = _____   7 + 7 = _____   5 + 8 = _____

Connect the dots in order. Start at 1.

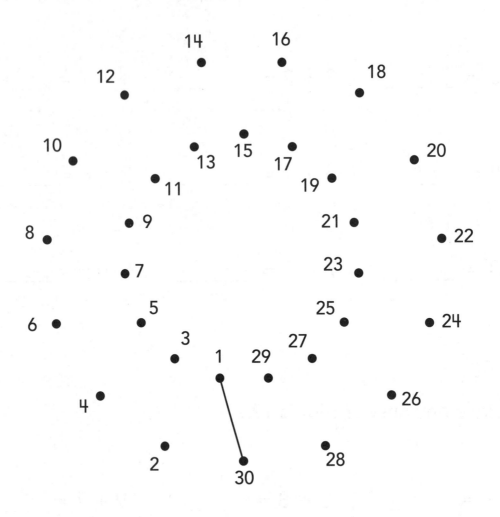

Write all the missing numbers.

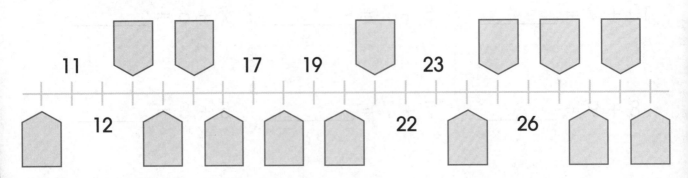

A big window has 25 panes (boxes).

1	2	3	4	5
6	7	8	9	10
11	12	13	14	15
16	17	18	19	20
21	22	23	24	25

Parts of the window are shown below.
Write in the missing numbers.

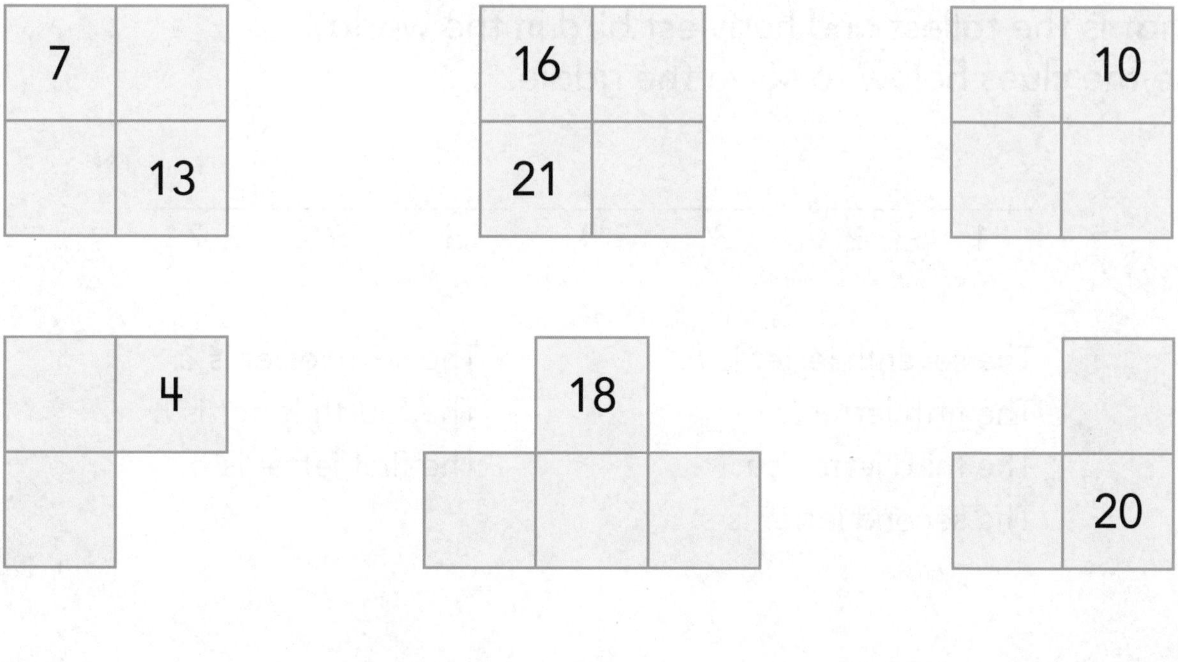

7	
	13

16	
21	

	10

	4

18

| | 20 |

Write 11 to 20 in order below the eggs.

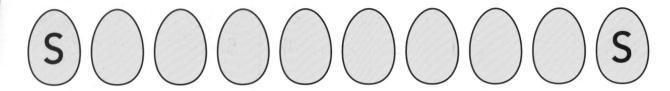

___ ___ ___ ___ ___ ___ ___ ___ ___ ___

Then write: A in the fourteenth egg L in the seventeenth egg
B in the sixteenth egg M in the fifteenth egg
C in the twelfth egg R in the nineteenth egg
E in the eighteenth egg and the thirteenth egg

What word did you spell? _____

....

What is the tallest and heaviest bird in the world?
Use the clues below to solve the riddle.

___ ___ ___ ___ ___ ___ ___
 1   2   3   4   5   6   7

The seventh letter is *h*. The sixth letter is *c*.
The fifth letter is *i*. The fourth letter is *r*.
The third letter is *t*. The first letter is *o*.
The second letter is *s*.

Draw what comes next in each pattern.

✖ ● ✖ ● ✖ ● ✖ _____ _____ _____ _____

♥ = ☾ ♥ = ☾ ♥ _____ _____ _____ _____

◇ ▲ ◇ ▲ ◇ ▲ ◇ ▲ ◇ _____ _____ _____ _____

Study the pattern in each row.
Draw the next shape for each pattern.

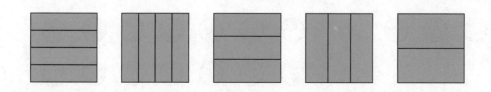

Circle pairs of objects in each group. Does the group have an odd number or an even number? Write *odd* or *even* on the line below each group.

1.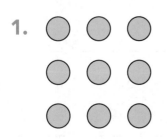

_____

2.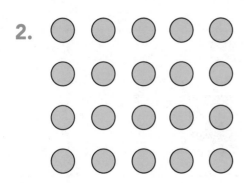

_____

3.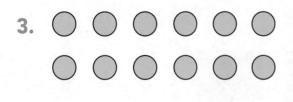

_____

4.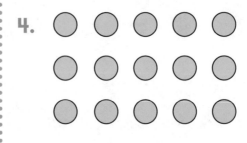

_____

5.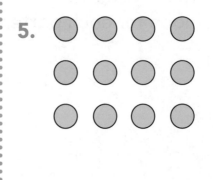

_____

6.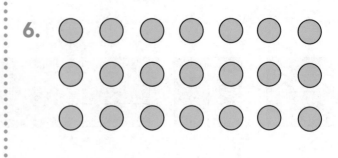

_____

Every number in the balloon is *odd* or *even*.
Write each number where it belongs.

Odd Numbers	Even Numbers

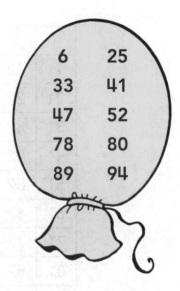

6   25
33   41
47   52
78   80
89   94

Color *odd* numbers RED. Color *even* numbers BLUE.
Color the empty spaces with colors of your choice.

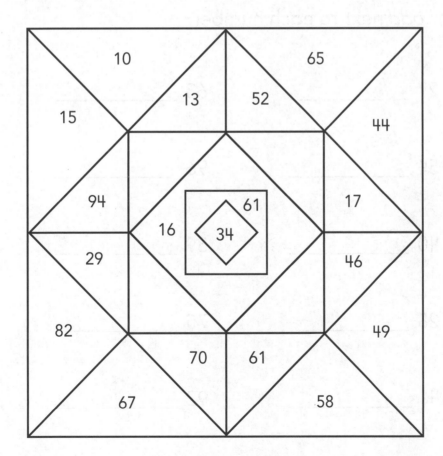

10   65
13   52
15   44
94   61   17
16   34
29   46
82   49
70   61
67   58

Shade in the even numbers on the chart.

1	2	3	4	5	6	7	8	9	10
11	12	13	14	15	16	17	18	19	20
21	22	23	24	25	26	27	28	29	30
31	32	33	34	35	36	37	38	39	40
41	42	43	44	45	46	47	48	49	50
51	52	53	54	55	56	57	58	59	60
61	62	63	64	65	66	67	68	69	70
71	72	73	74	75	76	77	78	79	80
81	82	83	84	85	86	87	88	89	90
91	92	93	94	95	96	97	98	99	100

Write *even* or *odd* next to each number.

27 _____   63 _____

54 _____   96 _____

40 _____   39 _____

28 _____   75 _____

41 _____   92 _____

Add doubles.

	4		8		6
+	4	+	8	+	6

	9		5		7
+	9	+	5	+	7

Now write the sums in order from *least* to *greatest*.

_____

Subtract. Think about doubles.

	18		12		16
−	9	−	6	−	8

	10		14		20
−	5	−	7	−	10

Now write the differences in order from *greatest* to *least*.

_____

Add. Circle the greatest sum.

$3 + 7 + 4 =$ _____ $5 + 2 + 6 =$ _____

$6 + 1 + 8 =$ _____ $9 + 6 + 4 =$ _____

$8 + 3 + 5 =$ _____ $5 + 9 + 4 =$ _____

Study the drawing. Find the sum of numbers:

1. inside the oval AND box. _____

2. inside the oval ONLY. _____

3. inside the box ONLY. _____

4. outside both shapes. _____

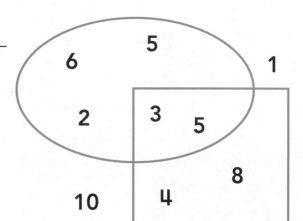

Figure out each code.

1. 🍂 + 🍂 = 10, so 🍂 = _____

2. 🌼 + 🌼 = 18, so 🌼 = _____

3. So, 🍂 + 🌼 = _____

4. And 🌼 – 🍂 = _____

5. 🥕 + 🥕 = 20, so 🥕 = _____

6. 🍄 + 🍄 = 14, so 🍄 _____

7. So, 🍄 + 🥕 = _____

8. And 🥕 – 🍄 = _____

Subtract. Circle all *even* answers.

10 – 2 = _____   8 – 6 = _____   7 – 1 = _____

9 – 7 = _____   6 – 5 = _____   10 – 3 = _____

8 – 5 = _____   7 – 4 = _____   9 – 5 = _____

Subtract. Circle all *odd* answers.

13 – 7 = _____   18 – 10 = _____   14 – 6 = _____

19 – 9 = _____   16 – 7 = _____   17 – 8 = _____

11 – 5 = _____   15 – 8 = _____   12 – 7 = _____

Write the number that comes just *after*.

36, _____   48, _____   53, _____

77, _____   80, _____   99, _____

Write the number that comes just *before*.

_____, 74   _____, 39   _____, 90

_____, 58   _____, 67   _____, 46

Write the number that comes *between*.

38, _____, 40   27, _____, 29   49, _____, 51

63, _____, 65   56, _____, 58   15, _____, 17

Add or subtract.
Circle the answer that is an *even* number.

$$\begin{array}{r} 7 \\ + \ 4 \\ \hline \end{array}$$

$$\begin{array}{r} 9 \\ - \ 6 \\ \hline \end{array}$$

$$\begin{array}{r} 8 \\ + \ 9 \\ \hline \end{array}$$

$$\begin{array}{r} 12 \\ - \ 7 \\ \hline \end{array}$$

$$\begin{array}{r} 5 \\ + \ 8 \\ \hline \end{array}$$

$$\begin{array}{r} 13 \\ - \ 9 \\ \hline \end{array}$$

Solve It

Show your work.

Linn has a rope 5 feet long. Kenya has a rope 7 feet long. The girls lay the ropes end-to-end. What is the total length?

_____

Show your work.

1. Tai invited 10 adults and 9 children to his party. But 2 adults and 3 children could not go. How many adults and how many children were at the party?

_____

2. Ruben had 13 dollars. He spent 5 dollars on a movie ticket and 2 dollars on popcorn. How much money did he have left?

_____ dollars

3. Dev buys a pen for $2, a hat for $4, and a book for $5. How much money does he spend in all? Dev spends

_____ .

4. Kiara has 6 butterfly stickers, 3 rainbow stickers, and 4 flower stickers. She gave 3 butterfly stickers to Jessie and 2 flower stickers to Allie. How many stickers does Kiara have left?

_____ .

Count by 2s to connect the dots.

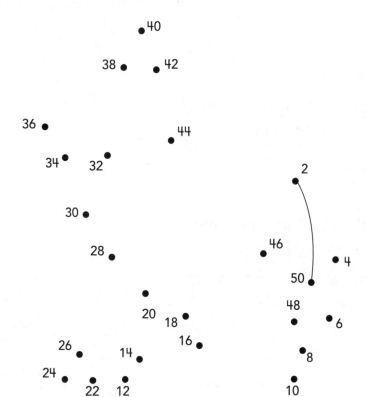

Skip count aloud by 5s. Write each number you say.

5, 10, ____, ____, ____, ____, ____,

____, ____, ____, ____, ____, ____,

____, ____, ____, ____, ____, ____, 100

Skip count by 10s to 100.

10, ____, ____, ____, ____,

____, ____, ____, ____, ____

Write each number.

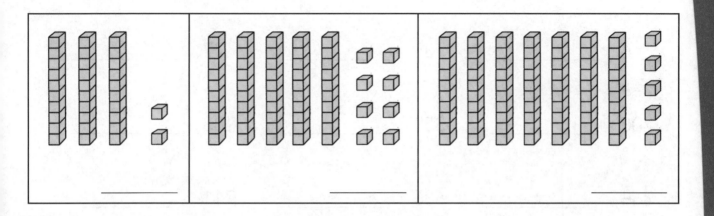

_____   _____   _____

Write the number on the line.

tens	ones
4	5

_____

tens	ones
3	1

_____

tens	ones
2	8

_____

tens	ones
6	7

_____

tens	ones
7	9

_____

tens	ones
5	0

_____

Write how many tens and ones.

72 = _____ tens _____ ones   90 = _____ tens _____ ones

45 = _____ tens _____ ones   63 = _____ tens _____ ones

89 = _____ tens _____ ones   31 = _____ tens _____ ones

Write the number that is 10 *more*.

6 _____   35 _____   77 _____

208 _____   354 _____   483 _____

364 _____   635 _____   711 _____

507 _____   882 _____   946 _____

Write the number that is 10 *less*.

13 _____   59 _____   86 _____

364 _____   450 _____   712 _____

135 _____   592 _____   867 _____

314 _____   420 _____   918 _____

Write the number form.

thirty   _____   forty-one   _____

fifty-three   _____   eighteen   _____

thirty-six   _____   ninety-nine   _____

Write the number for each clue.

A	B	▓	C	D
▓	E	F	▓	
▓	▓	G	H	▓
I		▓	J	

Across

A. forty-four

C. 20 + 3

E. 30 – 1

G. sixty-seven

I. 7 + 9

J. 8 tens + 3 ones

Down

B. 40 + 2

D. 40 – 2

F. ninety-six

H. seventy-eight

Write a number from the box for each clue.

1. I have 4 tens. _____

2. I have 6 ones. _____

3. I have no ones. _____

4. I have 8 tens. _____

5. I have the same number of
tens and ones. _____

6. Which number is not used? _____

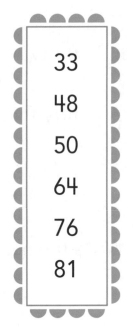

33

48

50

64

76

81

X the one in each row that does *not* belong.

7. 22	2 tens 2 ones	2 + 2	twenty-two
8. 53	5 tens 3 ones	50 + 3	thirty-five
9. 74	4 tens 7 ones	40 + 7	forty-seven
10. 81	1 ten 8 ones	80 + 1	eighty-one

Write in standard form. The first one has been done for you.

1. 3 tens 5 ones   <u> 35 </u>

2. 8 tens 1 one   <u>   </u>

3. 2 tens 6 ones   <u>   </u>

4. 9 tens 3 ones   <u>   </u>

5. 5 tens 7 ones   <u>   </u>

6. 6 tens 0 ones   <u>   </u>

7. 7 tens 8 ones   <u>   </u>

8. 4 tens 2 ones   <u>   </u>

Write in expanded form. The first one has been done for you.

9. 83   <u>   80 + 3   </u>

10. 56   <u>   </u>

11. 47   <u>   </u>

12. 35   <u>   </u>

13. 60   <u>   </u>

Add 40 to each number.

24 _____   53 _____   47 _____

Subtract 30 from each number.

98 _____   67 _____   84 _____

Add or subtract. Circle the greatest answer.

$$
\begin{array}{r} 80 \\ -\ 30 \\ \hline \end{array}
\qquad
\begin{array}{r} 40 \\ +\ 50 \\ \hline \end{array}
\qquad
\begin{array}{r} 80 \\ +\ 90 \\ \hline \end{array}
$$

$$
\begin{array}{r} 140 \\ -\ 70 \\ \hline \end{array}
\qquad
\begin{array}{r} 130 \\ -\ 50 \\ \hline \end{array}
\qquad
\begin{array}{r} 70 \\ +\ 60 \\ \hline \end{array}
$$

Add. Circle two sums that are the same.

$$\begin{array}{r} 13 \\ + \ 54 \\ \hline \end{array}$$

$$\begin{array}{r} 61 \\ + \ 17 \\ \hline \end{array}$$

$$\begin{array}{r} 39 \\ + \ 50 \\ \hline \end{array}$$

$$\begin{array}{r} 44 \\ + \ 53 \\ \hline \end{array}$$

$$\begin{array}{r} 53 \\ + \ 16 \\ \hline \end{array}$$

$$\begin{array}{r} 27 \\ + \ 42 \\ \hline \end{array}$$

Subtract. Circle the answer that has 9 ones.

$$\begin{array}{r} 76 \\ - \ 54 \\ \hline \end{array}$$

$$\begin{array}{r} 68 \\ - \ 25 \\ \hline \end{array}$$

$$\begin{array}{r} 59 \\ - \ 20 \\ \hline \end{array}$$

$$\begin{array}{r} 44 \\ - \ 13 \\ \hline \end{array}$$

$$\begin{array}{r} 83 \\ - \ 42 \\ \hline \end{array}$$

$$\begin{array}{r} 97 \\ - \ 61 \\ \hline \end{array}$$

Regroup 10 ones as 1 ten. The first one has been done for you.

1. 3 tens 12 ones = ___4___ tens ___2___ ones

2. 5 tens 11 ones = _____ tens _____ ones

3. 2 tens 18 ones = _____ tens _____ ones

4. 4 tens 14 ones = _____ tens _____ ones

5. 6 tens 13 ones = _____ tens _____ ones

6. 7 tens 17 ones = _____ tens _____ ones

Regroup 1 ten as 10 ones. The first one has been done for you.

7. 3 tens 2 ones = ___2___ tens ___12___ ones

8. 5 tens 6 ones = _____ tens _____ ones

9. 2 tens 7 ones = _____ tens _____ ones

10. 4 tens 4 ones = _____ tens _____ ones

11. 6 tens 3 ones = _____ tens _____ ones

12. 9 tens 1 ones = _____ tens _____ ones

Add. Regroup as needed. Circle the greatest sum.

$$\begin{array}{r} 48 \\ +\ 36 \\ \hline \end{array}$$ $$\begin{array}{r} 75 \\ +\ 16 \\ \hline \end{array}$$ $$\begin{array}{r} 51 \\ +\ 39 \\ \hline \end{array}$$

$$\begin{array}{r} 36 \\ +\ 49 \\ \hline \end{array}$$ $$\begin{array}{r} 40 \\ +\ 82 \\ \hline \end{array}$$ $$\begin{array}{r} 94 \\ +\ 53 \\ \hline \end{array}$$

Subtract. Regroup as needed. Circle the difference that is even.

$$\begin{array}{r} 45 \\ -\ 28 \\ \hline \end{array}$$ $$\begin{array}{r} 63 \\ -\ 14 \\ \hline \end{array}$$ $$\begin{array}{r} 55 \\ -\ 29 \\ \hline \end{array}$$

$$\begin{array}{r} 74 \\ -\ 37 \\ \hline \end{array}$$ $$\begin{array}{r} 81 \\ -\ 45 \\ \hline \end{array}$$ $$\begin{array}{r} 90 \\ -\ 63 \\ \hline \end{array}$$

Add or subtract. Regroup as needed.
Circle the 3-digit answer.

$$\begin{array}{r} 65 \\ -\ 29 \\ \hline \end{array}$$

$$\begin{array}{r} 74 \\ +\ 18 \\ \hline \end{array}$$

$$\begin{array}{r} 94 \\ +\ 20 \\ \hline \end{array}$$

$$\begin{array}{r} 70 \\ -\ 36 \\ \hline \end{array}$$

$$\begin{array}{r} 87 \\ -\ 59 \\ \hline \end{array}$$

$$\begin{array}{r} 19 \\ +\ 66 \\ \hline \end{array}$$

Solve It

Show your work.

Daria's book has 96 pages. She
read 28 pages on Monday. She
read 17 pages on Tuesday. How
many more pages are left to read?

_____ pages

Add. Regroup as needed. Circle the greatest sum.

$$
\begin{array}{r}
14 \\
37 \\
+\ 21 \\
\hline
\end{array}
\qquad
\begin{array}{r}
25 \\
52 \\
+\ 16 \\
\hline
\end{array}
\qquad
\begin{array}{r}
53 \\
51 \\
+\ 67 \\
\hline
\end{array}
$$

$$
\begin{array}{r}
28 \\
40 \\
+\ 27 \\
\hline
\end{array}
\qquad
\begin{array}{r}
53 \\
18 \\
+\ 25 \\
\hline
\end{array}
\qquad
\begin{array}{r}
29 \\
32 \\
+\ 16 \\
\hline
\end{array}
$$

Solve It

Show your work.

Lola picks 3 baskets of limes.
One basket has 25 limes. Another
basket has 22 limes. The third
basket has 20 limes. How many
limes has Lola picked in all?

_____

Round each number to the nearest ten.

24 → _____   57 → _____   15 → _____   81 → _____

72 → _____   43 → _____   69 → _____   96 → _____

Round each addend to the nearest ten. Then estimate the sum.

47 → ☐   31 → ☐   72 → ☐

+ 32 → ☐   + 28 → ☐   + 19 → ☐

about: _____   about: _____   about: _____

Round each number to the nearest ten. Then estimate the difference.

78 → ☐   62 → ☐   73 → ☐

− 33 → ☐   − 28 → ☐   − 17 → ☐

about: _____   about: _____   about: _____

Compare. Write < (less than) or > (greater than).

68 ◯ 86   37 ◯ 29   44 ◯ 40

7 ◯ 81   90 ◯ 85   23 ◯ 32

Order from *least* to *greatest.*

1. 30, 70, 55, 35 _____

2. 62, 67, 60, 70 _____

3. 73, 105, 200, 162 _____

Order from *greatest* to *least.*

4. 27, 72, 54, 45 _____

5. 49, 59, 29, 39 _____

6. 105, 250, 520, 55 _____

Show your work.

1. Van A has seats for 15 riders. Van B has seats for 16 riders. Van C has seats for 14 riders. How many seats are in Vans A and C?

_____ seats

2. Casey is a good baseball player. He threw a baseball 87 feet. Fern's best throw was 15 feet shorter. How far did Fern's best throw go?

_____ feet

3. A school chorus has 45 singers. There are 23 boys. How many of the singers are girls?

_____ girls

4. Ms. Davis put out 28 colored markers for her students. She has 34 more markers in the supply closet. How many markers does Ms. Davis have in all?

_____ markers

Show your work.

1. Dad is older than 40 and younger than 70. His age is an even number. Its digits add to 9. How old is Dad?

He is _____ years old.

....

2. Amos has 26 cards. Zadie has 18 cards. After Amos gives Zadie some cards, they both have the same number of cards. How many cards did Amos give Sadie?

_____

....

3. Otis raises cows and chickens. Cows have 4 legs. Chickens have 2 legs. One day, Otis counts 26 legs in the yard. He sees 1 more chicken than he sees cows. How many of each animal does Otis see?

Hints:
• Guess and check.
• Make a list.
• Draw a picture.

_____ chickens and

_____ cows

Show your work.

1. I am a 2-digit even number. I am less than 60. Add my digits to get 12. Subtract one of my digits from the other to get 4. What number am I?

   _____

2. I am a 3-digit number. The sum of my digits is 1. What number am I?

   _____

3. I am a 2-digit number. I am greater than 70. The digit in my tens place is even. The digit in my ones place is 3 less than the digit in my tens place. What number am I?

   _____

4. Write the next two numbers in each number pattern.

   Use this space to figure out the rules.

   2, 8, 14, 20, _____ , _____

   21, 32, 43, 54, _____ , _____

Long ago, people in Egypt drew pictures to stand for numbers. Write the number we use for the value of each picture number. Then write the picture number for our numbers.

1 =	Ι
10 =	∩
100 =	၁

1. ΙΙΙΙΙΙΙΙ = _____

2. ∩∩∩ ΙΙ = _____

3. ၁၁၁၁၁၁၁ = _____

4. ၁၁∩ΙΙΙΙΙΙ = _____

5. 14 = _____

6. 40 = _____

7. 200 = _____

8. 135 = _____

Count by hundreds.

100, _____ , 300, _____ , _____ ,

600, _____ , _____ , _____ , 1,000

Write all the missing numbers.

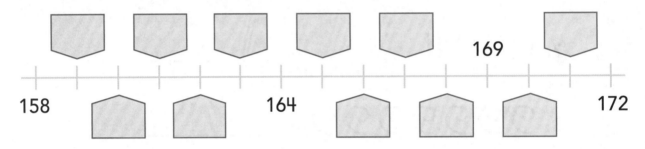

Write all the missing numbers.

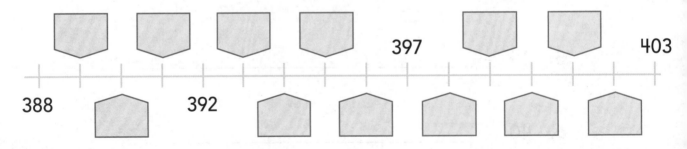

Count back by 100.

943, _____ , _____ , _____ , _____ ,

_____ , _____ , _____ , _____ , 43

Write the number that comes just *after*.

346, _____   480, _____   797, _____

808, _____   531, _____   959, _____

Write the number that comes just *before*.

_____ , 734   _____ , 139   _____ , 909

_____ , 528   _____ , 647   _____ , 460

Write the number that comes *between*.

245, _____ , 247   272, _____ , 274   147, _____ , 149

623, _____ , 625   564, _____ , 566   808, _____ , 810

479, _____ , 481   799, _____ , 801   966, _____ , 968

Write the number to show how many.

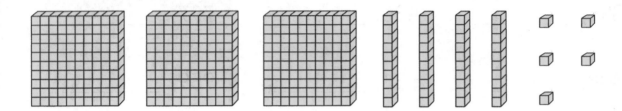

_____

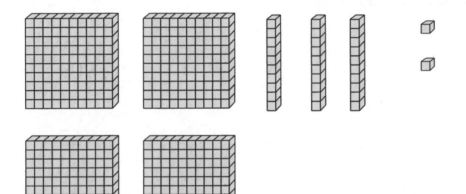

_____

Write the number on the line.

Hundreds	Tens	Ones
4	8	7

_____

Hundreds	Tens	Ones
9	1	4

_____

Hundreds	Tens	Ones
8	9	6

_____

Hundreds	Tens	Ones
5	0	2

_____

How many hundreds, tens, and ones?

1. 542 = _____ hundreds _____ tens _____ ones

2. 785 = _____ hundreds _____ tens _____ ones

3. 369 = _____ hundreds _____ tens _____ ones

4. 804 = _____ hundreds _____ tens _____ ones

5. 217 = _____ hundreds _____ tens _____ ones

6. 430 = _____ hundreds _____ tens _____ ones

Write in number form.

7. three hundred seventy-eight _____

8. four hundred thirty-nine _____

9. nine hundred ninety _____

10. five hundred sixty-one _____

11. six hundred eleven _____

12. one hundred five _____

Write in standard form.

1. 6 hundreds 3 tens 5 ones = _____

2. 8 hundreds 1 ten 4 ones = _____

3. 5 hundreds 7 tens 2 ones = _____

4. 3 hundreds 9 tens 0 ones = _____

5. 4 hundreds 2 tens 3 ones = _____

6. 7 hundreds 0 tens 9 ones = _____

Write each number in expanded form.

7. 734 = _____

8. 291 = _____

9. 568 = _____

10. 439 = _____

11. 686 = _____

12. 352 = _____

Add. Circle the sum that has digits in counting order.

$$341 + 517$$

$$632 + 145$$

$$396 + 502$$

$$444 + 253$$

$$827 + 162$$

$$234 + 555$$

Subtract. Circle the answer that has all digits the same.

$$948 - 517$$

$$674 - 201$$

$$832 - 512$$

$$765 - 543$$

$$579 - 146$$

$$826 - 116$$

Write the value of the underlined digit.

1. 6<u>2</u>8 _____

2. <u>6</u>04 _____

3. <u>7</u>50 _____

4. 14<u>9</u> _____

5. 89<u>3</u> _____

6. 3<u>8</u>5 _____

Write a number from the balloon for each clue.

7. I have **3** hundreds. _____

8. I have **7** tens. _____

9. I have no tens. _____

10. I have **5** ones. _____

11. I have as many ones as hundreds. _____

12. Which number is not used? _____

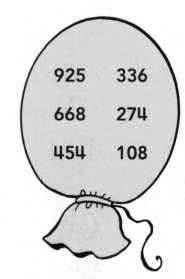

925   336

668   274

454   108

Regroup 10 tens as 1 hundred. The first one has been done for you.

1. 4 hundreds 16 tens = ___5___ hundreds ___6___ tens

2. 7 hundreds 17 tens = _____ hundreds _____ tens

3. 3 hundreds 15 tens = _____ hundreds _____ tens

4. 6 hundreds 14 tens = _____ hundreds _____ tens

5. 8 hundreds 18 tens = _____ hundreds _____ tens

Regroup 1 hundred as 10 tens. The first one has been done for you.

6. 5 hundreds 7 tens = ___4___ hundreds ___17___ tens

7. 8 hundreds 6 tens = _____ hundreds _____ tens

8. 2 hundreds 5 tens = _____ hundreds _____ tens

9. 4 hundreds 3 tens = _____ hundreds _____ tens

10. 9 hundreds 0 tens = _____ hundreds _____ tens

Add. Regroup 10 ones as 1 ten. Circle the *even* answers.

$$428 + 359$$

$$523 + 268$$

$$627 + 254$$

$$308 + 456$$

$$545 + 128$$

$$369 + 315$$

Add. Regroup 10 tens as 1 hundred. Circle the *odd* answers.

$$240 + 388$$

$$363 + 263$$

$$495 + 354$$

$$563 + 176$$

$$645 + 271$$

$$382 + 454$$

Round each number to the nearest hundred.

324 → _____   567 → _____   745 → _____   881 → _____

272 → _____   481 → _____   639 → _____   928 → _____

Round each addend to the nearest hundred. Estimate the sum.

471 → ☐   184 → ☐   528 → ☐
+ 316 → ☐   + 509 → ☐   + 382 → ☐

about: _____   about: _____   about: _____

Round each number to the nearest hundred. Estimate the difference.

643 → ☐   376 → ☐   851 → ☐
− 281 → ☐   − 125 → ☐   − 408 → ☐

about: _____   about: _____   about: _____

Add or subtract. Use mental math. Circle answers of 700.

400 + 500 = _____   1,000 – 300 = _____

700 – 200 = _____   800 – 200 = _____

300 + 600 = _____   200 + 500 = _____

Start at the left. Do what the arrow says
to find the next number. (Use the key.)
Write the number in the box.
Keep going to the end of the row.

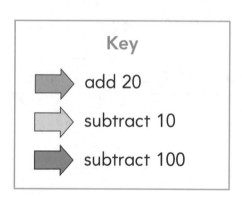

Key

add 20

subtract 10

subtract 100

543 ▢ ▢ ▢ ▢

862 ▢ ▢ ▢ ▢

791 ▢ ▢ ▢ ▢

Add. Regroup as needed. Circle the greatest sum.

```
   415          285          203
   239          312          181
+  141        + 160        + 545
```

```
   316          253          514
   481          193          368
+   52        + 212        + 107
```

Solve It

A band gave 3 shows. Friday's
show had 135 fans. Saturday's
show had 241 fans. Sunday's show
had 223 fans. How many fans in all
heard the band?

_____

Show your work.

Add or subtract. Regroup as needed. Circle the least answer.

$$
\begin{array}{r}
86 \\
-49 \\
\hline
\end{array}
\qquad
\begin{array}{r}
65 \\
+73 \\
\hline
\end{array}
\qquad
\begin{array}{r}
279 \\
-196 \\
\hline
\end{array}
$$

$$
\begin{array}{r}
345 \\
+638 \\
\hline
\end{array}
\qquad
\begin{array}{r}
462 \\
-207 \\
\hline
\end{array}
\qquad
\begin{array}{r}
501 \\
+289 \\
\hline
\end{array}
$$

Solve It

Which is the greater sum?

All of the numbers *outside* the circle or all of the numbers *outside* the triangle?

The numbers outside the

_____

have the greater sum.

How much greater? _____

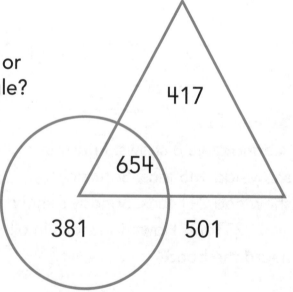

Subtract. Regroup as needed. Circle the *even* answers.

$$864 - 317$$ $$672 - 445$$ $$836 - 408$$

$$761 - 528$$ $$575 - 239$$ $$823 - 716$$

Subtract. Regroup as needed. Circle the *odd* answers.

$$867 - 597$$ $$648 - 175$$ $$719 - 365$$

$$936 - 486$$ $$585 - 294$$ $$404 - 122$$

Write a letter from the code to make each number sentence true.

| A = 30 | E = 10 | I = 20 | O = 40 | U = 50 | Y = 60 |

1. 74 + _____ = 94

2. _____ − 25 = 25

3. _____ + 38 = 68

4. 130 − _____ = 120

5. 7 + _____ = 47

6. 100 − 40 = _____

Use number sense. Figure out each missing digit.

```
   86
 - □4
 ----
   52
```

```
  □3
+ 68
----
  91
```

```
  □6
- 19
----
  57
```

```
  3□
+ 81
----
 120
```

```
  90
- 7□
----
  14
```

```
  4□
+ 25
----
  71
```

Compare. Write < (less than) or > (greater than).

681 ◯ 816   371 ◯ 317   402 ◯ 420

705 ◯ 689   908 ◯ 899   882 ◯ 891

Order from *least* to *greatest*.

1. 530, 405, 545, 354 _____

2. 819, 914, 814, 948 _____

3. 783, 875, 728, 857 _____

Order from *greatest* to *least*.

4. 462, 467, 470, 460 _____

5. 380, 308, 808, 838 _____

6. 265, 652, 526, 500 _____

Use each number in the oval.
Write it in the box where it belongs.
Then make up one more number for each box.

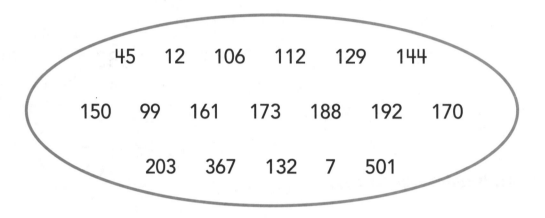

45   12   106   112   129   144

150   99   161   173   188   192   170

203   367   132   7   501

Numbers < 123	Numbers From 124 to 170	Numbers > 170

Show your work.

1. Walid is making a family album. So far, he has 86 photos of his parents. He also has 103 photos of his brothers and sisters. How many photos are in Walid's album?

_____ photos

2. A jet has 178 seats. There are 52 seats next to windows. The exit rows have 26 seats. How many other seats does the jet have?

_____ seats

3. A ferry boat can safely carry 85 cars. It can also carry 298 people. How many more people than cars can ride on the ferry?

_____ people

4. Daryl swam 75 yards in the pool. Hannah swam 125 yards. How many more yards did Hannah swim than Daryl?

_____ yards

Use these 4 number cards.
List *every* 3-digit number you can
make that is less than 583.
Write the numbers in the box.

| 8 | 3 | 0 | 5 |

Circle the *greatest* number. Underline the *least* number.

· ·

Use the number cards to write:

| 5 | 7 | 3 |

1. the greatest 3-digit number _____

2. the least 3-digit number _____

3. a number that rounds to 50 _____

4. a number that rounds to 700 _____

5. the number nearest to 400 _____

Color each fraction.

one third

one half

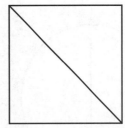

one fourth

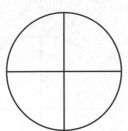

the whole

Write the fraction for each shaded part.

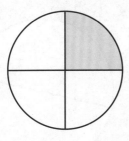

_____

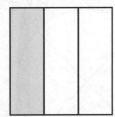

_____

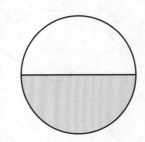

_____

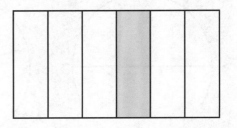

_____

For each circle, color *halves* red. Color *thirds* yellow.
Color *fourths* blue.

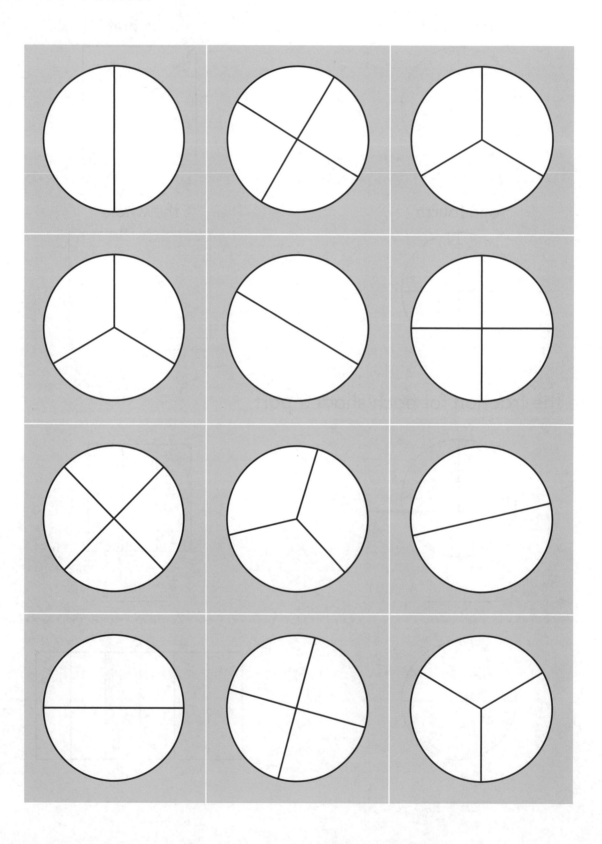

Add. Look for a pattern.

$3 + 3 =$ _____

$3 + 3 + 3 =$ _____

$3 + 3 + 3 + 3 =$ _____

So, what is five 3s? _____

$4 + 4 =$ _____

$4 + 4 + 4 =$ _____

$4 + 4 + 4 + 4 =$ _____

So, what is five 4s? _____

Add. Then find the product.

1. $2 + 2 + 2 + 2 =$ _____

   $4 \times 2 =$ _____

2. $5 + 5 =$ _____

   $2 \times 5 =$ _____

3. $6 + 6 + 6 =$ _____

   $3 \times 6 =$ _____

1. There are 50 sticky notes in every pack. Gary gets 4 packs. How many sticky notes does he have? Use mental math to solve. He has

_____ sticky notes.

Use this space if you need to.

2. A box is 25 inches tall. You stack up 3 boxes. How tall is your stack? The stack is

_____ inches tall.

Show your work.

3. Each ◆ = 1 dart. Write the score each dartboard shows.

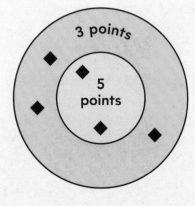

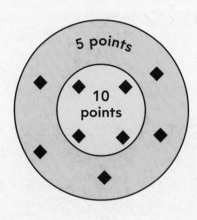

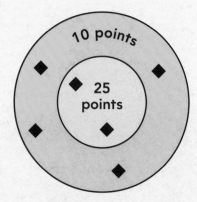

Score: _____   Score: _____   Score: _____

Show your work.

1. A flower shop makes spring tulip baskets. Each basket has 6 tulips. How many tulips are in 4 baskets?

There are _____ tulips in 4 baskets.

2. A spider has 8 legs. How many legs are there on 4 spiders?

_____ legs

3. A game needs teams of 4 children. There are 16 children who want to play. How many teams can be made?

_____ teams

4. A sports club has 25 players. The coach wants to make 5 equal teams. How many players will be on a team?

_____ players

For each batch of cookies, there are 20 raisins. Put the same number of raisins on each cookie. How many raisins are left over?

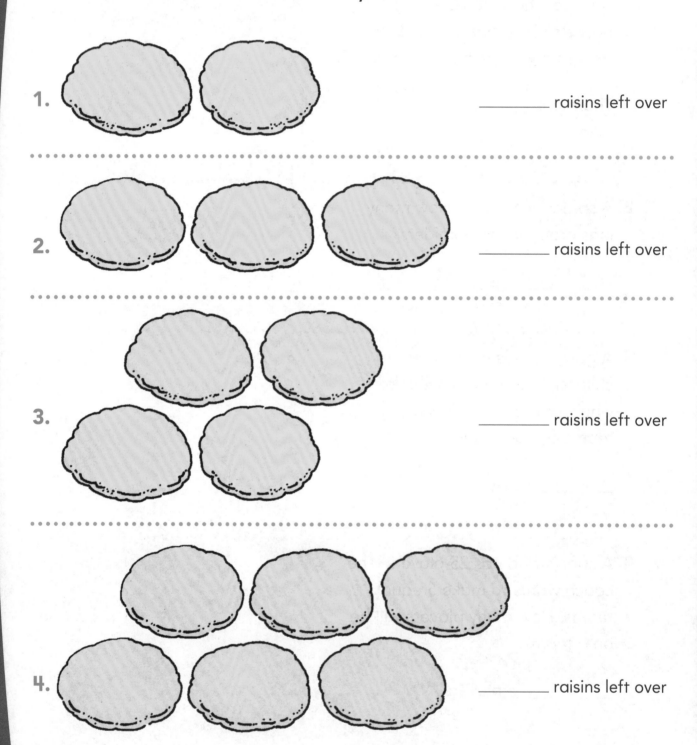

1. _____ raisins left over

2. _____ raisins left over

3. _____ raisins left over

4. _____ raisins left over

Put the same number of items in each group.
How many groups? Draw a picture to help you.

1. You have 12 beads.

Make groups of 6.

How many groups? _____

2. You have 15 hats.

Make groups of 5.

How many groups? _____

3. You have 14 pens.

Make groups of 7.

How many groups? _____

Divide. Make sure each group has the same number of things.

4. 16 fish   4 bowls

How many fish in each bowl? _____

5. 21 kids   3 teams

How many kids on each team? _____

6. 18 plums   6 jars

How many plums in each jar? _____

Use a 🖇 to measure each picture.
Measure to the nearest 🖇 .

_____

_____

_____

Stretch your hand wide. The length between your thumb
and pinky is called your hand *span*. You can use your hand
span to estimate and measure. Estimate first. Then measure in spans.

Distance	Estimate Spans	Measure Spans
Across a table		
Along your arm		
Across an open book		
Height of a chair		
Width of a bed		

Cut out the ruler below. Use it to measure the following lines. Record the length of each line.

1. _____ cm

2. _____ cm

3. _____ cm

4. _____ cm

5. _____ cm

6. _____ cm

7. _____ cm

8. _____ cm

9. _____ cm

10. _____ cm

Cut out the ruler below. Use it to measure the following shapes. Record the length of each shape. Then find the difference.

1.

Shape A

Shape B

Length of Shape A: _____ cm

Length of Shape B: _____ cm

Difference: _____ cm

2.

Shape C

Shape D

Length of Shape C: _____ cm

Length of Shape D: _____ cm

Difference: _____ cm

3.

Shape E

Shape F

Length of Shape E: _____ cm

Length of Shape F: _____ cm

Difference: _____ cm

4.

Shape G

Shape H

Length of Shape G: _____ cm

Length of Shape H: _____ cm

Difference: _____ cm

5.

Shape I

Shape J

Length of Shape I: _____ cm

Length of Shape J: _____ cm

Difference: _____ cm

cm
0 1 2 3 4 5 6 7 8 9 10 11 12 13 14 15 16 17

Write each money amount with a ¢ sign.

6 pennies = _____

5 dimes 7 pennies = _____

1 dime 4 pennies = _____

8 dimes 9 pennies = _____

3 dimes 5 pennies = _____

9 dimes = _____

4 dimes = _____

98 pennies = _____

Count the coins. Write how much.

1. _____ ¢

2. _____ ¢

3. _____ ¢

Round each money amount to the nearest dime.

27¢ _____   42¢ _____   66¢ _____   88¢ _____

34¢ _____   55¢ _____   71¢ _____   83¢ _____

Round each number to estimate the difference.

66¢ ⟶ ☐   42¢ ⟶ ☐   93¢ ⟶ ☐
− 42¢ ⟶ ☐   − 26¢ ⟶ ☐   − 48¢ ⟶ ☐
      _____   _____   _____

about: _____ ¢   about: _____ ¢   about: _____ ¢

Round to the nearest dollar. Estimate the difference.

$4.13 ⟶ ☐ $9.28 ⟶ ☐ $7.46 ⟶ ☐
− $1.77 ⟶ ☐   − $5.81 ⟶ ☐   − $3.99 ⟶ ☐
       _____   _____   _____

about: $ _____   about: $ _____   about: $ _____

Count the money. Write how much. Use $ and ¢.

1.

_____

2.

_____

3.

_____

4.

_____

5.

_____

6.

_____

You have 1 of each coin. How many different amounts can you make using just 2 coins? Using just 3 coins?

List all of the amounts below.
Draw pictures or use play coins to help you.

Money Amounts With 2 Coins	Money Amounts With 3 Coins

- -

Solve It

Terry has 7 coins. He has no quarters or pennies. He has 1 more of one kind of coin than of the other kind. How much money could Terry have? Find 2 different answers.

Show your work.

1. _____   2. _____

Look at the two sets of money. Circle the one that is worth more.

1.

2.

3.

4.

5.

Round each amount to the nearest dollar.

$1.33 → _____ $5.79 → _____ $2.35 → _____

$3.67 → _____ $4.28 → _____ $6.81 → _____

Add or subtract money. Circle the answers that round to $4.

$5.52 − $2.08	$3.78 + $1.81	$8.14 − $5.60
$6.95 + $2.43	$7.40 − $3.90	$4.85 + $3.28
$9.57 − $3.23	$2.18 + $6.32	$5.46 − $1.25

Show your work.

1. Eva found 25¢ under the sofa. Then her dad gave her 3 nickels and 1 dime. How much money does Eva have now?

_____

2. Lulu has 4 coins. They total 60¢. What coins does Lulu have?

She has _____

_____

_____

3. Gracie finds some coins in a drawer. They total 64¢. She has the same number of pennies, nickels, and dimes. How many of each kind of coin does she have?

_____

How much money would Gracie have if she found 1 *more* penny, nickel, and dime?

_____

Show your work.

1. Ruthie went to a diner for lunch. She spent $3.29 for a sandwich and $1.50 for lemonade. How much did Ruthie spend on lunch?

_____

2. Kiri bought a hamburger for $1.50, salad for $1.20, and iced tea for $1.00. How much did she spend in all?

Kiri spent _____ in all.

3. Jake took 5 quarters and 6 dimes to the store. He spent 85¢ on a fruit roll. He spent 50¢ on a banana. How much money does Jake have left?

Jake has _____ left.

4. Leah is going with her dad to visit her grandma. They're taking the train. The child ticket costs $3.00. The adult ticket costs $5.75. How much do both tickets cost?

_____

Bryant loves bread products! Use the menu to answer the questions.

Breakfast Breads

Bagel With Butter	$1.10
Bagel With Cheese	$1.40
Cinnamon Toast	$ .75
Corn Muffin	$1.20
English Muffin	$ .85
Honey Biscuit	$ .60
Texas Toast	$1.50

1. How much would Bryant spend for 3 honey biscuits? _____

2. How much more is a bagel with cheese

than a bagel with butter? _____

3. Bryant gets an English muffin and cinnamon toast.

How much does he spend? _____

4. Bryant spends $2.90 for 2 items. What are they?

_____ and _____

5. Bryant pays $2 for a corn muffin. How much change should he get back?

_____

Write each time with A.M. or P.M.

Draw hands to show each time.

quarter to 3

half past 10

30 minutes after 5

Solve It

Show your work.

A baker starts work at 6:00 A.M.
He ends work at 3:00 P.M.
How many hours does the baker work?

He works _____ hours.

Write the time shown on each clock.

_____

_____

_____

_____

_____

_____

_____

_____

_____

Read the story. Draw clock hands to show what time things happened. Then answer the question.

> At 1:00 the first guest came. In a few minutes everyone was there. At 1:30 we went outside to run races.
>
> We ran three relay races. In the first race, you had to keep an egg on your spoon while you ran. That took about 15 minutes. The next race was the funniest. Each group had a bag of clothes. We had to put on all the clothes before we could run. That race lasted a half hour. Then we had a skipping relay.
>
> At 2:30 we had lemonade and watermelon. By 3:00 the party was over.

1. 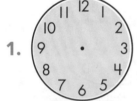 first guest comes   2.  egg race begins

3. 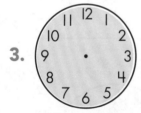 clothes race begins   4. 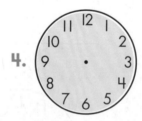 skipping race begins

5.  lemonade and watermelon

6. How long did the party last? _____ hours

Use the picture graph to answer questions about Lee's fish.

Lee's Fish

Kind of Fish

Angel

Molly

Tetra

1 2 3 4 5

Number of Fish

1. How many different kinds of fish does Lee have? _____

2. Lee has _____ angel fish.

3. Lee has 2 _____ fish.

4. Lee has _____ more tetra fish than angel fish.

5. Lee has _____ fish in all.

Use the graph about rainy days to answer the questions.

Rainy Days

August	🌂 🌂 🌂
September	🌂 🌂
October	🌂 🌂 🌂 🌂 🌂
	Key: 🌂 = 2 days

1. Which month was the rainiest? _____

2. What does 1 umbrella mean? _____

3. How many rainy days were there in August? _____

4. How many rainy days were there in September? _____

5. How many more rainy days were there in October than in August?

   _____

Use the table about animal teeth to answer the questions.

How Many Teeth?

Animal	Teeth
Alligator 🐊	🦷🦷🦷🦷🦷🦷🦷🦷 🦷🦷🦷🦷🦷🦷🦷🦷
Beaver 🦫	🦷🦷🦷🦷
Horse 🐴	🦷🦷🦷🦷🦷🦷🦷🦷🦷
Lion 🦁	🦷🦷🦷🦷🦷🦷
	Key: 🦷 = 5 teeth

1. How many teeth is each  ? _____

2. How many teeth does a lion have? _____

3. Which animal has 80 teeth? _____

4. Which animal has half the number of teeth as the alligator?

_____

5. How many teeth do the beaver and horse have altogether? _____

Mara's class learned about wild birds that live near the school. The children picked the bird they like best. Mara made a graph to show the votes. Use the graph to answer the questions.

Wild Birds

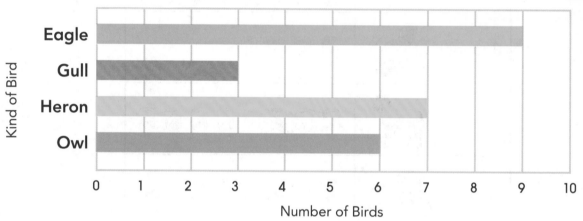

Kind of Bird

Number of Birds

1. Which bird got the most votes? _____

2. How many children voted for that bird? _____

3. Which bird got 6 votes? _____

4. Which bird got the least votes? _____

5. How many more children voted for the heron than the owl? _____

Use the graph about people's favorite footwear to answer
the questions.

Favorite Footwear

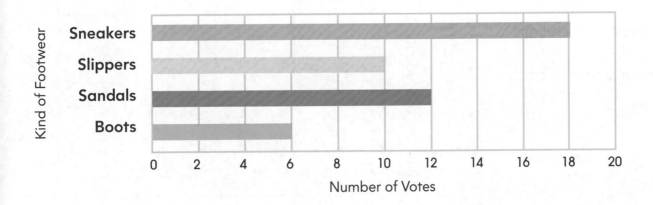

1. How many people like boots best? _____

2. How many people like sandals best? _____

3. How many more like sandals than slippers? _____

4. Which 2 kinds of footwear got as many votes as sneakers?

    _____ and _____

5. How many votes are there in all? _____

This is how Mr. Hay's students got to school today.

- Six took the bus.

- Five walked.

- Three rode bikes.

- Four came in cars.

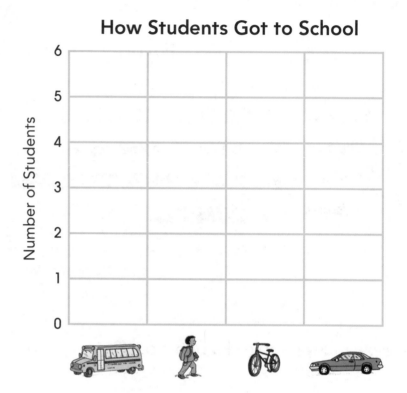

How Students Got to School

Number of Students

Way of Getting to School

Graph the data. Then answer these questions.

1. How many students got to school today? _____

2. How many more walked than came in cars? _____

3. Which way did most students get to school? _____

4. How many more took the bus than rode bikes? _____

5. How many students took the bus and came in cars? _____

Unscramble the shape words.
Use the word bank to check
your spelling.

Word Bank

circle	cone	cube
hexagon	rectangle	sphere
square	triangle	

bceu _____

enoc _____

qarsue _____

crilec _____

preesh _____

langerit _____

noxhage _____

grancleet _____

Draw the shapes.
Start and stop each line at a dot.

Triangle   Rectangle   Hexagon

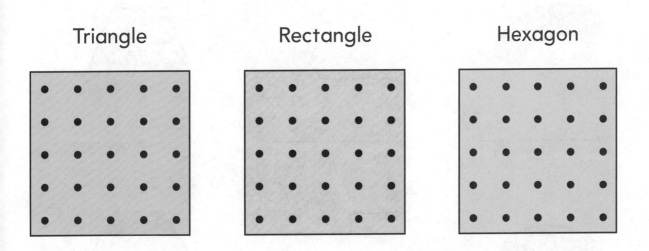

A **polygon** is a closed shape that has straight sides. Some of these shapes are polygons. Others are not. Write *yes* if the shape is a polygon and *no* if it is not a polygon.

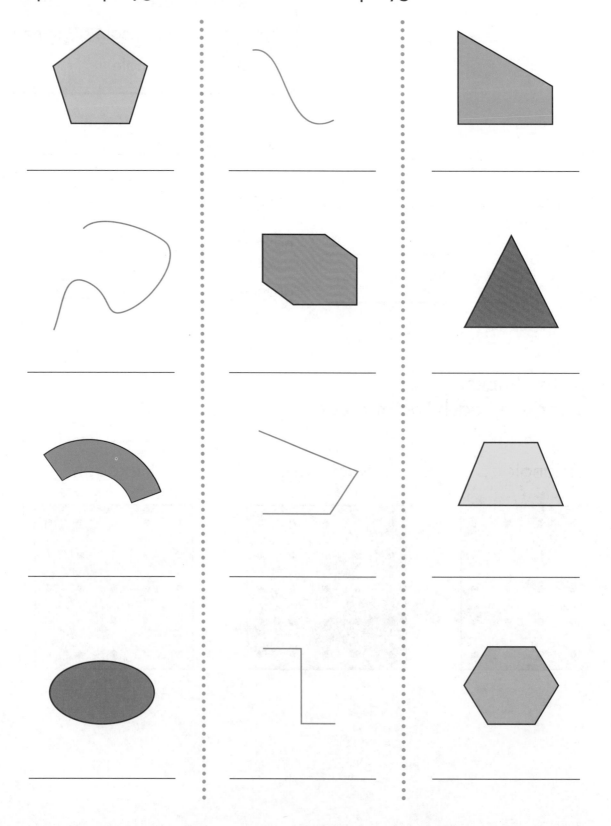

Each of these shapes is a triangle (has 3 sides), a quadrilateral
(4 sides), a pentagon (5 sides), or a hexagon (6 sides).
Label each shape.

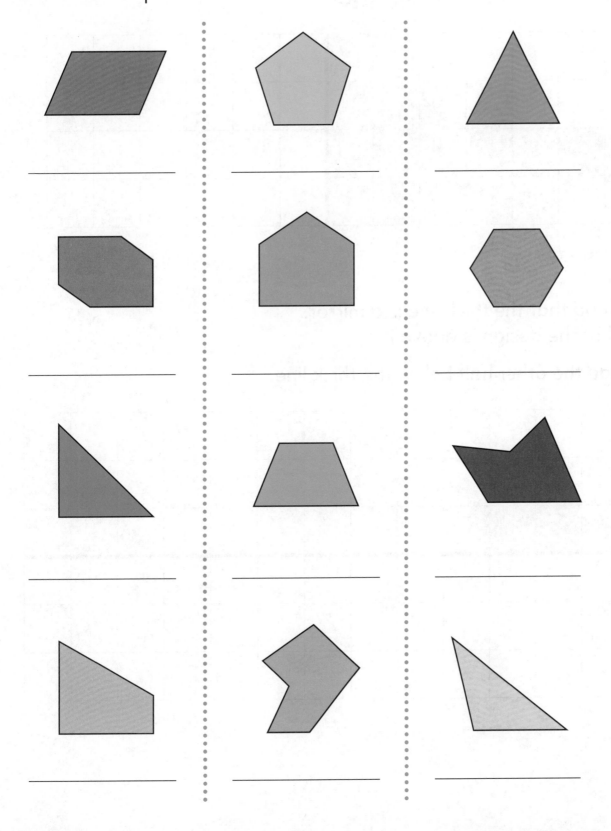

Pretend that the thick line is a mirror.
Half of the design is on the left.

Shade the other half on the right.

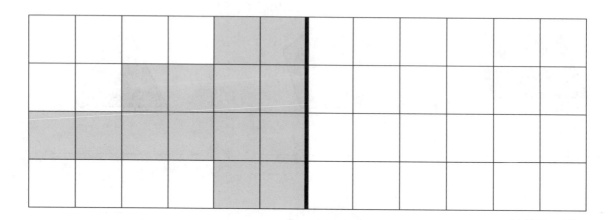

Pretend that the thick line is a mirror.
Half of the design is above it.

Shade the other half below the thick line.

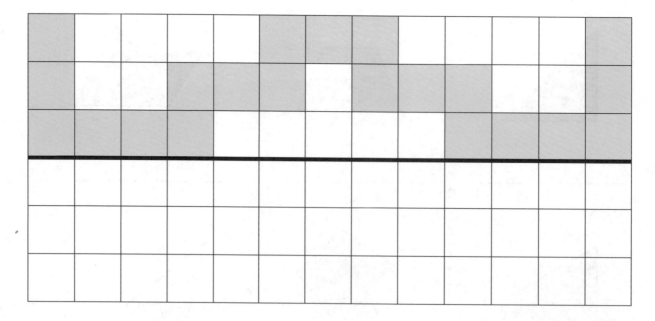

Answer Key

PHONICS

p. 10
1. b 4. f
2. h 5. v
3. d 6. m

p. 11
1. s 4. t
2. k 5. f
3. b 6. d

p. 12
1. b 4. l
2. g 5. p
3. v 6. r

p. 13
1. B 4. E
2. M 5. E
3. B 6. M

p. 14
1. m 5. n
2. r 6. m
3. n 7. n
4. m 8. r

p. 15
1. e 4. a
2. a 5. i
3. e 6. u

p. 16
Possible answers:
–ack: back, hack, knack, lack, pack, quack, rack, sack, tack, clack, crack, shack, slack, smack, snack, stack, track, whack
–ap: cap, gap, lap, map, nap, rap, sap, tap, yap, chap, clap, flap, scrap, slap, snap, strap, trap, wrap
–ank: bank, lank, rank, sank, tank, yank, blank, clank, crank, drank, flank, plank, prank, spank, thank
–ash: bash, cash, dash, gash, hash, lash, mash, rash, sash, brash, clash, crash, flash, slash, smash, stash, thrash, trash
–at: bat, cat, fat, gnat, hat, mat, pat, rat, sat, vat, brat, chat, flat, scat, slat, spat, that
–an: ban, can, fan, man, pan, ran, tan, van, bran, clan, plan, scan, span, than

p. 17
Possible answers:
–ell: bell, cell, dell, fell, jell, sell, tell, yell, dwell, shell, smell, spell, swell
–ent: bent, cent, dent, gent, lent, rent, sent, tent, vent, went, scent, spent
–est: best, jest, lest, nest, pest, rest, test, vest, west, zest, blest, chest, crest, quest, wrest
–ess: guess, less, mess, bless, chess, dress, press, stress
–eck: deck, heck, neck, peck, check, fleck, speck, wreck
–ed: bed, fed, led, red, wed, bled, bred, fled, shed, shred, sled, sped

p. 18
Possible answers:
–ick: kick, lick, pick, quick, sick, tick, wick, chick, click, flick, slick, stick, thick, trick, wick
–ink: kink, link, mink, pink, rink, sink, wink, blink, brink, clink, drink, shrink, slink, stink, think
–ill: ill, bill, dill, fill, gill, hill, kill, mill, pill, quill, sill, till, will, chill, drill, frill, grill, skill, spill, still, thrill, trill, twill
–itch: ditch, hitch, pitch, witch, switch
–ing: bing, ding, king, ping, ring, sing, wing, zing, bring, cling, fling, sling, spring, sting, string, swing, thing, wring
–ig: big, dig, fig, gig, jig, pig, rig, wig, brig, sprig, swig, twig

p. 19
Possible answers:
–ock: dock, hock, knock, lock, mock, rock, sock, tock, clock, crock, flock, frock, shock, smock, stock
–og: bog, cog, dog, fog, hog, jog, log, clog, flog, frog, smog
–op: bop, cop, hop, mop, pop, sop, top, chop, crop, drop, flop, plop, prop, shop, slop, stop
–ox: ox, box, fox, lox, pox
–ob: cob, gob, job, knob, lob, mob, rob, sob, blob, glob, slob, snob, throb
–ot: cot, dot, got, hot, jot, knot, lot, not, pot, rot, tot, blot, clot, plot, shot, slot, spot, trot

p. 20
Possible answers:
–uck: buck, luck, muck, puck, suck, tuck, cluck, pluck, stuck, struck, truck
–unk: bunk, dunk, hunk, junk, sunk, chunk, drunk, flunk, plunk, shrunk, skunk, slunk, spunk, stunk, trunk
–ug: bug, dug, hug, jug, lug, mug, pug, rug, tug, chug, drug, plug, shrug, slug, smug, snug, thug
–ush: gush, hush, lush, mush, rush, blush, brush, crush, flush, plush, slush, thrush
–ump: bump, dump, hump, jump, lump, pump, rump, chump, clump, frump, grump, plump, slump, stump, thump, trump
–ub: cub, dub, hub, nub, rub, sub, tub, club, flub, grub, scrub, shrub, snub, stub

p. 21
2. weep, deep
3. Fred, bread
7. bench, French
8. swift, lift

p. 22
1. can; possible answer: take
2. pan; possible answer: tail
3. had; possible answer: gray
4. gal; possible answer: late

p. 23
1. sell; possible answer: meal
2. bend; possible answer: tree
3. set; possible answer: need
4. tent; possible answer: peel

p. 24
1. lick; possible answer: rice
2. bread; possible answer: tide
3. kit; possible answer: night
4. tray; possible answer: dry

p. 25
1. box; possible answer: moat
2. spot; possible answer: woke
3. cow; possible answer: low
4. bun; possible answer: cone

310

p. 26
1. tube; possible answer: lube
2. blue; possible answer: true
3. mute; possible answer: cute
4. chew; possible answer: threw

p. 27
1. suit 2. two 3. roof 4. soup

p. 28
Long *a*: flake, tray
Long *e*: free, heat
Long *i*: sigh, pie, child
Long *o*: foam, both
Long *u*: fruit, tune, cute

p. 29
o͞o as in *moon*: fool, school, tooth, spoon, room
o͝o as in *book*: cook, hood, foot, good, look

p. 30
1. car, shore
2. thorns, sharp
3. corn, farm
4. sport, hard
5. horse, smart

p. 31
h<u>er</u>d: germ, fern, verb, serve
b<u>ir</u>d: girl, stir, first, shirt
n<u>ur</u>se: curl, burn, fur, hurt

p. 32
1. long *i*   5. long *i*
2. long *e*   6. long *i*
3. long *e*   7. long *e*
4. long *i*   8. long *e*

p. 33
1. alarm   5. awake
2. again   6. asleep
3. adult   7. ago
4. agree   8. about

p. 34
1. H   5. H
2. S   6. S
3. H   7. H
4. S   8. H

p. 35
1. H   5. S
2. S   6. S
3. S   7. S
4. H   8. H

p. 36
1. groom   5. drift
2. fresh   6. drapes
3. crisp   7. trust
4. brook   8. prank

p. 37
1. pl   5. bl or sl
2. fl or pl   6. cl, fl, or sl
3. cl or gl   7. bl or gl
4. bl or gl   8. bl, cl, fl, or gl

p. 38
1. small   5. scare
2. swim   6. spoil
3. sleeve   7. smart
4. star   8. slow

p. 39
1. de<u>sk</u>   5. qui<u>lt</u>   9. bi<u>rd</u>
2. gi<u>ft</u>   6. ha<u>nd</u>   10. sha<u>rk</u>
3. sta<u>mp</u> 7. dri<u>nk</u> 11. che<u>st</u>
4. co<u>ld</u>   8. te<u>nt</u>   12. wa<u>sp</u>

p. 40
1. ch   4. th
2. sh   5. wh
3. ph   6. sh
7. gh   10. ng
8. ph   11. th
9. ch   12. sh

p. 41
1. boil, enjoy, point
2. royal, coin, voice
3. Joyce, Troy, Leroy
4. shout, howl, cloud
5. meow, crown, pout, flower
6. allow, ouch, loud

p. 42
Answers will vary.
Possible answers: 1. <u>ch</u>in 2. <u>sh</u>oe
3. <u>pr</u>ize 4. <u>sn</u>eeze 5. <u>tr</u>ick
6. <u>cl</u>own 7. <u>th</u>ing 8. <u>sp</u>ot
9. <u>wh</u>ite 10. <u>dr</u>ink

READING COMPREHENSION

p. 45
1. A 2. B 3. C 4. A

p. 47
1. B 2. B 3. A 4. C

p. 49
1. C 2. A 3. B 4. A

p. 51
1. B 2. B 3. A 4. C

p. 53
1. C 2. A 3. B 4. A

p. 55
1. C 2. B 3. A 4. A

p. 57
1. A 2. C 3. B 4. A

p. 59
1. A 2. C 3. A 4. C

p. 61
1. B 2. A 3. B 4. D

p. 63
1. C 2. B 3. D 4. C

p. 65
1. B; Sample answer: The story says Goran was in bed with the flu, so he was sick (lines 2–3).
2. D; Sample answer: The story says that winds can spin very fast, like a tornado. So, I picked the word most like *spins* (lines 18–19).
3. Sample answer: Mama was testing how warm he felt to see if he had a fever.
4. Sample answer: A mystery has something you don't know but have to figure out. This story is about the mystery of raining frogs (lines 18–22).

p. 67

1. B; Sample answer: The author says that the breaker room was as hot as an oven (lines 6–7).
2. A; Sample answer: His family needed money (lines 18–20), so he had to make the boss think he was old enough (lines 1–3).
3. Sample answer: A breaker boy takes out everything that isn't coal (lines 9–12).
4. Sample answer: Boys are sitting on wooden benches. They are picking through coal (lines 6, 9–12) while bent over (lines 15–17).

p. 69

1. B; Sample answer: Midas cried, "NO MORE!" because his daughter turned into a statue. He couldn't take it anymore and was sad (lines 19–22).
2. A; Sample answer: In line 7, I read that he loved his new power. So I think *giddy* means "joyful."
3. Sample answer: He was already the richest person on Earth (lines 1–3). Plus, everything turned to gold, so there was nothing to eat or drink (lines 13–17).
4. Sample answer: He went to bed hungry the night before (lines 16–17), and he was really happy his daughter was okay again (lines 24–25).

p. 71

1. C; Sample answer: It says in lines 1 and 2 that most people say that unicorns aren't real, so that's why I picked C.
2. D; Sample answer: The unicorn said A and B (lines 7 and 9), but those aren't about telling the truth. So I picked D, which is about truth (lines 15–16).
3. Sample answer: I think it means the hair on the outside of the body. In the picture, the unicorn has a mane and a tail and looks like a horse. And a horse's body is covered with hair.

4. Sample answer: Except for eating cobwebs, each secret has some good ideas in it. It's good to be clean (lines 7–8), to drink milk (lines 9–10), to exercise (lines 13–14), to look into people's eyes when they speak (lines 15–16), and to pick your friends carefully (lines 17–20).

p. 73

1. C; Sample answer: I counted the number of different meanings, and there are five (line 19).
2. A; Sample answer: I read all the choices, and only A wasn't there (lines 10–20).
3. Sample answer: Meaning 5 fits the sentence best. In that meaning and in the sentence, *mine* is used in the same way (lines 19–20).
4. Sample answer: Meaning 2—a large tunnel or space made in the earth to dig out valuable things—fits the sentence best. Copper is something they dug out of that old mine (lines 13–14).

p. 75

1. B; Sample answer: I know that this poster is about what to do in an emergency, so B is a good answer. The other choices don't fit.
2. C; Sample answer: An emergency is something very serious. In lines 8–10, it says to call 9-1-1 only if someone is hurt or in danger. Fire, bad falls, and deep cuts are emergencies. A squirrel in an attic is not.
3. Sample answer: It ends when the operator says it's OK to hang up (lines 36–37).
4. Sample answer: The 9-1-1 operator will ask questions to find out details about what's wrong (lines 16–20, 23–28). So if you stay calm and speak clearly, you can say the important stuff (lines 31–34) and get the right help as soon as possible.

p. 77

1. C; Sample answer: I read that Jerry Pinkney knew he was using his mind when he was drawing (lines 19–20).
2. D; Sample answer: I read that Jerry Pinkney has been a book illustrator for more than 50 years, and he made the art for more than 100 books (lines 2–5).
3. Sample answer: Jerry Pinkney didn't read as well as the other kids did, no matter how hard he tried (lines 16–18).
4. Sample answer: He believes that mistakes are a new chance to do better, and he works with a pencil and an eraser all the time (lines 24–26).

p. 79

1. B; Sample answer: I found three of the four idioms in the essay (lines 3, 8, 13–14), so I picked the one that wasn't there.
2. A; Sample answer: I read each choice and figured out which one was backward, or in the wrong order (lines 17–23).
3. Sample answer: An idiom is a saying. The words in it can stand for something different than what you think they mean (lines 1–5).
4. Sample answer: I think *horse sense* is like common sense because, of course, you zip your jacket after you put it on (lines 19–20).

p. 80

guess, mittens, shovel, wiggle, nodded

Think About It! Sample answer: Brian likes to play guessing games and is funny.

p. 81

history, special, salute, praise, proudly

Think About It! Sample answer: People fly the flag on special days and to show their pride for their country.

p. 82
freezing, gusts, drifts, uncover, swirling
Think About It! Sample answer: In a regular snowstorm, it snows for only a few hours. But in a blizzard, it can snow for several hours and even days. Strong gusts of wind can create mounds of snow that bury cars.

p. 83
communicate, attention, greeting, different, stretches
Think About It! Sample answer: Pearl meows to say hello or to get attention. She also purrs to show she's happy, and rubs against her owner's leg to let him know she's hungry. She also rolls on her back and stretches to show that she trusts her owner.

p. 84
huge, flowed, ceiling, underwater, floating
Think About It! Sample answer: Sun and Moon's house was flooded when Sea came to visit, so they had to move to the sky.

p. 85
waiting, video, married, comb, cavity, surprise
Think About It! Sample answer: The dentist does silly things so that kids are not afraid when they go to see him.

p. 86
invented, watched, tumbled, amusing, machine
Think About It! Sample answer: He got the idea for the Slinky when he saw a large spring fall off a shelf, roll over a table, and tumble to the floor.

p. 87
beneath, terrified, thundering, solid, laughed
Think About It! Sample answer: The hare heard a loud noise and felt the ground shake, so he thought that meant the earth was breaking apart.

p. 88
giant, Millions, helium, Volunteers, directors
Think About It! Sample answer: Dozens of gigantic balloons float in the air, held down by volunteers holding ropes. Crowds of people watch in the streets, and millions more watch on TV.

p. 89
gadgets, adult, construct, clothespin, mobiles
Think About It! Sample answer: Calder was creative, artistic, and imaginative. He was also a hard worker.

p. 90
amazing, underground, chambers, repaired, system, dynamite
Think About It! Sample answer: Ant and termite homes are built to protect the insects and their families. Ant homes are built underground, while termite homes are above ground.

WRITING

p. 126
1. gate
2. toe
3. wink or eye
4. joey
5. arm
6. fire or flame

p. 127
1. bun
2. cloud
3. gas pump
4. wing
5. log or fireplace
6. stamp

p. 128
1. The cat is old. OR, Is the cat old?
2. Where are my slippers?
3. Let's bake some cookies.
4. This book is too hard. OR, Is this book too hard?
5. Who knows the right answer?

p. 129
1. C 2. B 3. D 4. B 5. C
6. A 7. D 8. C 9. D 10. D

p. 130
1. thing 2. place 3. persons
4. idea 5. person 6. persons
7. thing 8. idea 9. things
10. idea 11. person 12. idea

p. 131
1. I ate a spicy pepper.
2. The eagle flew so high.
3. That old kite lost its tail.
4. You need a hammer to fix it.
5. She likes the book's red jacket.
6. Let's make a play castle.

p. 132
1. panda or bear 2. bear or panda 3. Jane 4. dog 5. wagon 6. birds

p. 133
1. children 2. car 3. clown
4. shoes 5. band 6. music

p. 134
Plural nouns: boys, dolls, lions, posters, balloons, balls, caps, shirts, hands

p. 135
1. dresses 2. sandwiches 3. foxes
4. dishes 5. buses 6. guesses
7. brushes 8. beaches 9. boxes
10. bushes

p. 136
1. She swings the bat.
2. They blow their whistles.
3. We warm up.
4. He looks for his glove.
5. It rolls into the field.

p. 137
1. c 2. a 3. d 4. a 5. c
6. b 7. b 8. c 9. d 10. a

p. 138
Answers will vary; check the use of verbs.

p. 139
1. C 2. B 3. C 4. C 5. A
6. B 7. A 8. C 9. B 10. B

p. 140

1. sit 2. digs 3. sells 4. run
(Pictures should show the actions
described in the sentences.)

p. 141

Possible answers: 1. gallops
2. stretches 3. splashes 4. rings
5. chews 6. spots 7. blares
8. sketches 9. slithers

p. 142

Verbs to replace: lost, boiled,
sprinkled, chewed, disappeared,
will push, dropped, opened,
waited, reach
Possible answer:
Alice <u>saw</u> the bread in the kitchen.
She <u>toasted</u> the bread. Then she
<u>spread</u> jam on it. Alice <u>drank</u> some
juice too.
The schoolbus <u>appeared</u> at the
corner.
"Alice, you <u>will miss</u> the bus!"
So Alice quickly <u>put</u> on her coat.
She <u>packed</u> her books into her
knapsack and <u>ran</u> out the door.
"Here I <u>come</u>!"

p. 143

cooks	cooked	cooking
tests	tested	testing
acts	acted	acting
orders	ordered	ordering
paints	painted	painting

raises	raised	raising
smiles	smiled	smiling
describes	described	describing
erases	erased	erasing
wiggles	wiggled	wiggling

p. 144

1. a 2. b 3. b 4. a 5. b
6. b 7. a 8. c 9. b 10. c

p. 145

2. blow 3. drank 4. dug
5. brought 6. forget 7. leave
8. seen 9. told 10. wrote

p. 146

Possible answers: 1. waits for a
mouse. 2. eats cheese. 3. sleeps.
4. has a ball. 5. rolls away.
6. spills.

p. 147

Answers will vary.

p. 148

1. C 2. B 3. C 4. A 5. D
6. C 7. A 8. C 9. A 10. C

p. 149

Answers will vary.

p. 150

Answers will vary.

p. 151

higher	highest
smaller	smallest
safer	safest
sillier	silliest
newer	newest
colder	coldest
earlier	earliest
darker	darkest
braver	bravest

p. 152

2. oldest 3. bigger 4. bluer
5. shorter 6. funnier 7. happier
8. busier 9. harder 10. tallest

p. 153

1. how much 2. how 3. where
4. how often, how 5. how
6. when 7. when

p. 154

1. sometimes, always, or usually
2. sometimes, always, or usually
3. quickly or hungrily 4. loudly
5. sometimes, always, or usually

p. 155

can't/cannot; didn't/did not; isn't/
is not; doesn't/does not; haven't/
have not; wouldn't/would not;
aren't/are not

p. 156

I'll/I will; they'll/they will; it'll/it
will; I've/I have; you've/you have;
we've/we have; let's/let us

p. 157

1. midle 2. barje 3. No mistake
4. fraktion 5. No mistake
6. explane 7. dinnor 8. No
mistake 9. blankit 10. lether
11. childrun 12. meself 13. No
mistake 14. gardin 15. monky

p. 158

1. H, h 2. d, D 3. R, r 4. l, L
5. w, W 6. t, T 7. i, I 8. S, s

p. 159

1. ? 2. ! 3. . 4. ? 5. ! 6. ?
7. . 8. ! 9. ? 10. ! or .

p. 160

Answers will vary. Sample answers:
1. Kim makes a snowman.
2. Mark brings sticks and a hat.
3. The snowman has arms.
4. The birds talk to the snowman.
5. They built a snow dog.

p. 161

1. Who put this basket here?
2. What is inside the basket?
3. What does Ben hear?
4. What does Ben see?
5. Who gave Ben a puppy?

p. 162

Answers will vary. Sample answers:
1. I have the balloon. 2. Why did
he take my balloon? 3. I will get
you a new one. 4. What are they
saying? 5. Do they have nuts?
6. I want one too.

p. 163

Drawings and ideas will vary.

p. 164

1. baseball; Sample answer:
What things do you need to play
baseball?
2. breakfast; Sample answer: Some
foods are popular for breakfast.

p. 165
1. dog; Sample answer: If you have a dog, here are some things you might need.
2. Answers will vary.

p. 166
Answers will vary.

p. 167
A. (top to bottom, left to right)
2, 4, 3, 1
B. 2, 4, 1, 3; Sample answers: Kate went to the library. She chose a book from the shelf. She checked out the book from the library. Kate enjoys reading the book.

p. 168
A. 1. 2, 4, 3, 1   2. 2, 3, 4, 1
B. 3, 2, 4, 1; Sample answers: Derek and Sara went into the pool. They splashed around. They saw some ducks nearby. The ducks jumped into the pool to play.

p. 169
Sample answers:
Writing Purpose: To tell a story about Nate's eggs.
Opening Sentence: Nate's family has some hens.
Sentences in Order: Each morning Nate goes to the henhouse. He collects eggs. Nate's mother cooks the eggs. Nate eats fresh eggs for breakfast.

p. 170
Answers will vary.

p. 171
Answers will vary.

p. 172
1. A 2. C 3. B 4. A 5. C
6. B 7. C 8. A

VOCABULARY

p. 175
A. 1. glide 2. wish 3. keep
4. shut 5. argue 6. exit
B. 1. slip 2. creep 3. wind
4. face

p. 177
1. hefty 2. cozy 3. sleepy
4. puzzled 5. damp 6. bright
7. grumpy 8. simple 9. breezy
10. icy

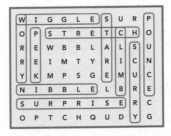

p. 179
A. 1. smile 2. yell 3. frown
4. laugh 5. whisper 6. hide
7. wreck
B. 1. weep 2. fix 3. show

p. 181
light/dark; tiny/huge; bland/spicy; early/late; loud/quiet

p. 183
A. 1. take 2. rest 3. creep
4. grab 5. spin 6. turn
B. 1. soup 2. eggs 3. park
4. bedroom

p. 185
1. stare 2. nibble 3. wiggle
4. surprise 5. scurry 6. worry
7. pounce 8. peek 9. climb
10. stretch

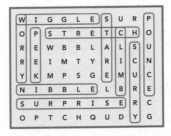

p. 187
1. gaze 2. crawl 3. fasten
4. sprinkle 5. scoot 6. yank
7. twist 8. soar 9. flutter 10. fade
Puzzle answer: action word

p. 189
A. 1. furry 2. foamy 3. wrinkled
4. slimy 5. creamy 6. sharp
B. 1. beach 2. tree bark 3. cookie
4. gum

p. 191
1. chirp 2. plink 3. splash
4. click 5. crackle 6. quack
7. achoo 8. whoosh 9. squeak
10. ding

p. 193
A. 1. sail 2. hole 3. sale
4. wrap 5. whole 6. pear
B. 1. two 2. knock 3. take
4. skyscraper

p. 195
A. 1. row 2. bat 3. ball
4. pitcher, ball 5. sign 6. row
B. 1. no 2. yes 3. yes

p. 197
1. cowboy 2. drumstick
3. wristwatch 4. sunflower
5. wheelchair 6. toothbrush
7. starfish 8. scarecrow
9. firefly 10. birdhouse

p. 199
1. snowflake 2. goldfish
3. headphones 4. wallpaper
5. clothespin 6. greenhouse
7. playground 8. sidewalk
9. grasshopper 10. houseboat

p. 201
A. 1. reuse 2. reread 3. untrue
4. remake 5. unhappy 6. unsafe
B. 1. story 2. after a trip
3. broken toy 4. crooked

p. 203
1. singer 2. joyful 3. painter
4. playful 5. baker 6. careful
7. hopeful 8. writer 9. colorful
10. builder

p. 205
A. 1. honest 2. gentle 3. fair
4. polite 5. curious 6. brave
B. 1. take 2. smile 3. bully
4. tiptoe

p. 207
Across: 3. breakfast 4. lunch
5. kitchen 7. dinner 9. dessert
Down: 1. drink 2. cafeteria
4. leftovers 6. snack 8. meal

p. 209
A. 1. visit 2. hotel 3. travel
4. vacation 5. camp 6. sleepover
B. 1. passport 2. ticket 3. map
4. suitcase

p. 211
Land words: cave, hill, mountain, dune, range
Water words: ocean, river, lake, pond, stream

p. 213
Path should go through these weather words in order: dust storm, hail, thunderstorm, blizzard, tornado, heat wave, flood, hurricane, sleet, fog

p. 215
A. 1. polar bear 2. elephant
3. camel 4. zebra 5. tiger
6. panda
B. 1. leopard 2. gorilla
3. rhinoceros 4. giraffe

p. 217
1. leaves 2. worm 3. shovel
4. mower 5. bloom 6. grass
7. hose 8. soil 9. rake 10. bush

p. 219
A. 1. penny 2. nickel 3. dime
4. quarter 5. half-dollar
6. dollar bill
B. 1. price 2. cash 3. change
4. coin

p. 221
Units of measure: centimeter, mile, foot, meter, inch, yard
Tools used to measure: ruler, meter stick, yardstick
Word not used: measure

MATH

p. 224

8	3
5	4
9	1
7	6
10	2

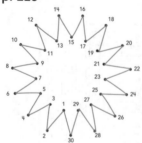

p. 225

6	5	8
7	6	8
9	9	10

11	16	16
19	12	13
17	14	13

p. 226

p. 227

7	8
12	13

16	17
21	22

9	10
14	15

p. 228
SCRAMBLERS
ostrich

p. 229

p. 230
1. Odd 2. Even 3. Even
4. Odd 5. Even 6. Odd

p. 231
Odd Numbers: 25, 33, 41, 47, 89
Even Numbers: 6, 52, 78, 80, 94

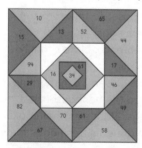

p. 232

1	2	3	4	5	6	7	8	9	10
11	12	13	14	15	16	17	18	19	20
21	22	23	24	25	26	27	28	29	30
31	32	33	34	35	36	37	38	39	40
41	42	43	44	45	46	47	48	49	50
51	52	53	54	55	56	57	58	59	60
61	62	63	64	65	66	67	68	69	70
71	72	73	74	75	76	77	78	79	80
81	82	83	84	85	86	87	88	89	90
91	92	93	94	95	96	97	98	99	100

odd	odd
even	even
even	odd
even	odd
odd	even

p. 233

8	16	12
18	10	14

8, 10, 12, 14, 16, 18

9	6	8
5	7	10

10, 9, 8, 7, 6, 5

p. 234

14	13
15	(19)
16	18

1. 8   2. 13   3. 12   4. 11

p. 235

1. 5   2. 9   3. 14   4. 4
5. 10   6. 7   7. 17   8. 3

p. 236

(8)	(2)	(6)
(2)	1	7
3	3	(4)

6	8	8
10	(9)	(9)
6	(7)	(5)

p. 237

37	49	54
78	81	100

73	38	89
57	66	45

39	28	50
64	57	16

p. 238

11	3	17
5	13	(4)

Solve It: 12 feet

p. 239

1. 8 adults and 6 children
2. 6 dollars   3. $11   4. 8 stickers

p. 240

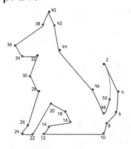

15, 20, 25, 30, 35,
40, 45, 50, 55, 60, 65,
70, 75, 80, 85, 90, 95

20, 30, 40, 50,
60, 70, 80, 90, 100

p. 241

32	58	75

45	31	28
67	79	50

7 tens 2 ones   9 tens 0 ones
4 tens 5 ones   6 tens 3 ones
8 tens 9 ones   3 tens 1 ones

p. 242

16	45	87
218	364	493
374	645	721
517	892	956

3	49	76
354	440	702
125	582	857
304	410	908

p. 243

30	41
53	18
36	99

p. 244

1. 48   2. 76   3. 50   4. 81
5. 33   6. 64   7. 2 + 2   8. thirty-five
9. 74   10. 1 ten 8 ones

p. 245

2. 81   3. 26   4. 93   5. 57
6. 60   7. 78   8. 42   10. 50 + 6
11. 40 + 7   12. 30 + 5   13. 60 + 0

p. 246

64	93	87
68	37	54

50	90	(170)
70	80	130

p. 247

67	78	89
97	(69)	(69)

22	43	(39)
31	41	36

p. 248

2. 6 tens 1 one   3. 3 tens 8 ones
4. 5 tens 4 ones   5. 7 tens 3 ones
6. 8 tens 7 ones   8. 4 tens 16 ones
9. 1 ten 17 ones   10. 3 tens
14 ones   11. 5 tens 13 ones
12. 8 tens 11 ones

p. 249

84	91	90
85	122	(147)

17	49	26
37	(36)	27

p. 250

36	92	(114)
34	28	85

Solve It: 51 pages

p. 251

72	93	(171)
95	96	77

Solve It: 67 limes

p. 252

20	60	20	80
70	40	70	100

50	30	70
30	30	20
80	60	90

80	60	70
30	30	20
50	30	50

p. 253

<	>	>
<	>	<

1. 30, 35, 55, 70
2. 60, 62, 67, 70
3. 73, 105, 162, 200
4. 72, 54, 45, 27
5. 59, 49, 39, 29
6. 520, 250, 105, 55

p. 254
1. 29 2. 72 3. 22 4. 62

p. 255
1. 54 2. 4 cards
3. 5 chickens and 4 cows

p. 256
1. 48 2. 100 3. 85
4. 26, 32; 65, 76

p. 257
1. 8 2. 32 3. 700 4. 216
5. ∩IIII 6. ∩∩∩∩
7. 𝟡 𝟡 8. 𝟡∩∩∩IIII

p. 258
200, 400, 500, 700, 800, 900

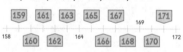

843, 743, 643, 543,
443, 343, 243, 143

p. 259

347	481	798
809	532	960

733	138	908
527	646	459

246	273	148
624	565	809
480	800	967

p. 260
345 432

487	914
896	502

p. 261
1. 5 hundreds 4 tens 2 ones
2. 7 hundreds 8 tens 5 ones
3. 3 hundreds 6 tens 9 ones
4. 8 hundreds 0 tens 4 ones
5. 2 hundreds 1 tens 7 ones
6. 4 hundreds 3 tens 0 ones
7. 378 8. 439 9. 990
10. 561 11. 611 12. 105

p. 262
1. 635 2. 814 3. 572
4. 390 5. 423 6. 709
7. 700 + 30 + 4 8. 200 + 90 + 1
9. 500 + 60 + 8 10. 400 + 30 + 9
11. 600 + 80 + 6 12. 300 + 50 + 2

p. 263

858	777	898
697	989	789

431	473	320
222	433	710

p. 264
1. 20 2. 600 3. 700 4. 9 5. 3
6. 80 7. 336 8. 274 9. 108
10. 925 11. 454 12. 668

p. 265
2. 8 hundreds 7 tens
3. 4 hundreds 5 tens
4. 7 hundreds 4 tens
5. 9 hundreds 9 tens
7. 7 hundreds 16 tens
8. 1 hundred 15 tens
9. 3 hundreds 13 tens
10. 8 hundreds 1 ten

p. 266

787	791	881
(764)	673	(684)

628	626	(849)
(739)	916	836

p. 267

300	600	700	900
300	500	600	900

500	200	500
300	500	400
800	700	900

600	400	900
300	100	400
300	300	500

p. 268

900	(700)
500	600
900	(700)

443 → 463 → 483 → 473
852 → 752 → 742 → 762
781 → 771 → 791 → 691

p. 269

795	757	929
849	658	(989)

Solve It: 599 fans

p. 270

(37)	138	83
983	255	790

Solve It: The numbers outside the circle have the greater sum; 36

p. 271

547	227	(428)
233	(336)	107

270	(473)	354
450	(291)	282

p. 272

1. I 2. U 3. A 4. E 5. O 6. Y

3	2	7
9	6	6

p. 273

<	>	<
>	>	<

1. 354, 405, 530, 545
2. 814, 819, 914, 948
3. 728, 783, 857, 875
4. 470, 467, 462, 460
5. 838, 808, 380, 308
6. 652, 526, 500, 265

p. 274

Numbers < 123	Numbers From 124 to 170	Numbers > 170
45	129	173
12	144	188
106	150	192
112	161	203
99	170	367
7	132	501

p. 275

1. 189 2. 100 3. 213 4. 50

p. 276

305, 308, 350, 358, 380, 385, 503, 508, 530, 538, (580)

1. 753 2. 357 3. 53
4. 735 5. 375

p. 277

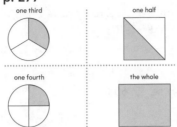

one third — one half — one fourth — the whole

1/4	1/3
1/2	1/6

p. 278

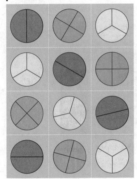

p. 279

6	8
9	12
12	16
15	20

1. 8, 8 2. 10, 10 3. 18, 18

p. 280

1. 200 2. 75 3. 19, 65, 90

p. 281

1. 24 2. 32 3. 4 4. 5

p. 282

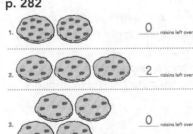
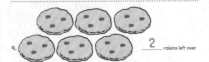

1. 0 raisins left over
2. 2 raisins left over
3. 0 raisins left over
4. 2 raisins left over

p. 283

1. 2 2. 3 3. 2
4. 4 fish 5. 7 kids 6. 3 plums

p. 284

Answers will vary depending on length of paper clip.
Answers will vary.

p. 285

1. 6 2. 4 3. 8 4. 3 5. 10
6. 2 7. 14 8. 12 9. 11 10. 17

p. 286

1. A: 3 B: 8 Difference: 5
2. C: 5 D: 7 Difference: 2
3. E: 2 F: 5 Difference: 3
4. G: 6 H: 6 Difference: 0
5. I: 7 J: 15 Difference: 8

p. 287

6¢	57¢
14¢	89¢
35¢	90¢
40¢	98¢

1. 89¢ 2. 72¢ 3. 66¢

p. 288

30¢	40¢	70¢	90¢
30¢	60¢	70¢	80¢

70¢	40¢	90¢
40¢	30¢	50¢
30¢	10¢	40¢

$4	$9	$7
$2	$6	$4
$2	$3	$3

p. 289

1. $3.93 2. $1.79 3. $2.80
4. $1.63 5. $3.52 6. $4.80

p. 290

2 coins: 6¢, 11¢, 26¢, 15¢, 30¢, 35¢
3 coins: 16¢, 31¢, 36¢, 40¢

Solve It: 55¢, 50¢

p. 291
1. 65¢ 2. $1.05 3. 85¢
4. 45¢ 5. 80¢

p. 292

$1	$6	$2
$4	$4	$7

$3.46	$5.59	$2.54
$9.38	($3.50)	$8.13
$6.34	$8.50	($4.21)

p. 293
1. 50¢
2. 2 quarters, 2 nickels
3. 4 of each coin; 80¢

p. 294
1. $4.79 2. $3.70 3. 50¢ 4. $8.75

p. 295
1. $1.80 2. $.30 more 3. $1.60
4. Texas Toast and Bagel With Cheese 5. $.80

p. 296
2:30 A.M.   6:45 A.M.   1:15 P.M.

Solve It: 9

p. 297

1:30	6:45	10:20
11:10	4:40	2:15
9:30	3:05	2:00

p. 298
1.   2.   3.
4.   5.

6. 2 hours

p. 299
1. 3 2. 3 3. molly 4. 2 5. 10

p. 300
1. October 2. 2 rainy days
3. 6 4. 4 5. 4

p. 301
1. 5 2. 30 3. Alligator
4. Horse 5. 60 teeth

p. 302
1. Eagle 2. 9 3. Owl 4. Gull 5. 1

p. 303
1. 6 2. 12 3. 2
4. Sandals and boots 5. 46

p. 304

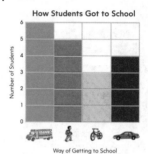

1. 18 2. 1 3. Bus 4. 3 5. 10

p. 305

cube	sphere
cone	triangle
square	hexagon
circle	rectangle

Drawings may vary, but check to make sure each shape is correct.

p. 306
From left to right, top to bottom:
yes; no; yes; no; yes; yes; no; no; yes; no; no; yes

p. 307
From left to right, top to bottom:
quadrilateral; pentagon; triangle; hexagon; pentagon; hexagon; triangle; quadrilateral; pentagon; quadrilateral; hexagon; triangle

p. 308

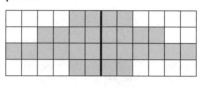

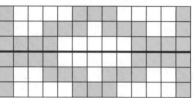